M000012021

Dancing

on My

Father's

Shoes

DANCING
on My
FATHER'S
SHOES

HEARTWARMING STORIES
to celebrate DAD

Guideposts
New York, New York

Dancing on My Father's Shoes

ISBN-10: 0-8249-4860-2
ISBN-13: 978-0-8249-4860-3

Published by Guideposts
16 East 34th Street
New York, New York 10016
Guideposts.org

Distributed by Ideals Publications, a Guideposts company
2630 Elm Hill Pike, Suite 100
Nashville, TN 37214

Guideposts and *Ideals* are registered trademarks of Guideposts.

Acknowledgments

Every attempt has been made to credit the sources of copyrighted material used in this book. If any such acknowledgment has been inadvertently omitted or miscredited, receipt of such information would be appreciated.

Acknowledgments are continued on pages 211 and 212, which are considered an extension of this copyright page.

"A Father, a Son, and an Answer" by Bob Greene is reprinted with permission from *Reader's Digest* and Tribune Media Services. © Tribune Media Services. All rights reserved.

"A Father's Blessing" by Morgan Cryar is reprinted from *Decision* magazine, June 1998; ©1998 Billy Graham Evangelistic Association; used by permission, all rights reserved.

"A Lesson from the Mound" by Beth Mullally is reprinted with permission from *Reader's Digest* and Times Herald Record.

"Asking for Forgiveness" by Luis Palau is reprinted with permission from *Calling America and Nations to Christ*, 1994, by Luis Palau Association.

"Barcelona Olympic 1992" by Ivan Maisel is reprinted with permission of *The Dallas Morning News*.

Library of Congress Cataloging-in-Publication Data has been applied for.

Edited by Elizabeth Kramer Gold
Cover by Black Kat Design
Cover photo by Getty Images
Interior design by Müllerhaus
Typeset by Aptara

Printed in the United States of America
10 9 8 7 6 5 4 3 2 1

CONTENTS

DEFINING DAD

LIFE LESSONS

$\mathscr{A}$ Father's Day Prayer

Jo Ann Heidbreder

Mender of toys, leader of boys,

Changer of fuses, kisser of bruises,

Bless him, dear Lord.

Wiper of noses, pruner of roses,

Singer of songs, righter of wrongs,

Guide him, O Lord.

Mover of couches, soother of ouches,

Pounder of nails, teller of tales,

Reward him, O Lord.

Hanger of screens, counsellor of teens,

Fixer of bikes, chastiser of tykes,

Help him, O Lord.

Raker of leaves, cleaner of eaves,

Dryer of dishes, fulfiller of wishes...

Bless him, O Lord.

INTRODUCTION

Da-da, Dad, Father, Pop—one man can go by a lot of names. In this volume, you'll meet fathers of all shapes and sizes.

There's the dad who teaches his daughter to dance by putting her tiny feet on his shoes as they waltz around the living room. There are several dads who forgive careless accidents as they recall their own misguided behavior. Fathers take the time to listen, to teach, to laugh, and to build memories of a lifetime. One dad does double time as dad *and* mom—and wants both a Mother's and Father's Day card.

There are stories by fathers who have learned, sometimes painfully, about being a father. The look in their children's eyes, or a carefully crayoned message, says it all.

Some dads earn the position as they arrive as stepdads, and they come to find a place in their children's hearts as permanent as if they were there on the day of their birth.

There are more than fifty true stories in this book—and yet there are thousands more stories out there of fathers who've secured a place in the hearts of their families. Enjoy.

Remembering with Love

The greatest gift I ever had
came from God; I call him Dad!

~Author Unknown

Sizzle
Margaret McSweeney

"Sizzle." That word is one of the most important lessons that my dad taught me in life. He was a Renaissance Man, a lyric tenor who recorded an album with the Concert Orchestra of London, a Fellow of the Royal Society of the Arts, an accomplished chef, a college president, a loving father, and one of my closest friends. My dad lived his life with vibrancy, a heart for God and others, and yes, with "sizzle."

When I was nine, my dad taught me how to dance for a school play about Martha Washington. My mother transformed a bathrobe into elegant eighteenth-century attire. My dad and I practiced the waltz for hours as I stepped on his toes and tripped on mine. He counted the steps over and over again in a gentle voice: "One, two, three…one, two, three." His kindness and patience along with those dance steps still echo in my heart today.

Each morning, my dad would tell me, "Something good is going to happen to you today." He was the ultimate believer in the power of positive thinking. Yet how could he not be that way? At age thirty, four years before I was born, my dad was diagnosed with malignant colon cancer that had metastasized.

In the late 1950s, my dad had few options other than extreme surgery. The doctor advised him to put his papers in order because he most likely would not even survive the surgery.

He and my mother were about to announce their decision to become missionaries overseas. Yet after this devastating news of cancer, my dad called the head of the Foreign Missionary Board and said, "Please pray for me." My dad recovered from the grueling surgery, and the cancer was removed. Weeks later my dad heard that missionaries around the world had formed a "prayer chain" and lifted up my dad to the Great Physician. He was healed.

As an awkward teenager, I spent many weekends at home without dates. My dad would insist on taking me out on a "Daddy/Daughter Date." After a gourmet meal at the Club in Birmingham, Alabama, he would lead me to the dance floor where we waltzed. Gliding across the floor, my dad would whisper, "You are such a beautiful young woman. Your mother and I are so proud of you." Those words instilled confidence and helped me navigate those challenging years. I'll never forget finding a note in the eighth grade hallway floor written by a boy that I liked. On this piece of paper, he referred to me as "an ugly dog." Those words stung but didn't penetrate through the protective barrier of self-assuredness that my dad had helped build.

My final dance with my dad was during my Poinsettia Debutante Ball. Taller and less awkward, I was a young woman dressed in a flowing white gown who waltzed in her father's arms. The next morning, my dad went on a business trip; yet he wrote me a special letter that I still have:

My dearest daughter Meg,

Somehow this morning I feel especially close to you—even though thousands of miles separate us. As I sit here on this snowy, cold morning in Israel, and as I reflect back upon the events of the past few days, the hustle and bustle of Christmastide 1982, the trip to Birmingham and the Poinsettia Ball with its beauty and significance, I somehow wanted to take a few moments and write on a heart-to-heart basis and communicate with you. As a father I must tell you how lovely you were on Tuesday evening at the Ball. You literally radiated a loveliness and charm as you moved so easily from group to group and person to person. How proud I am to observe you in action and to realize my little gal has moved into beautiful young womanhood—and...that she has learned the important lesson of life—**making others feel important**. Beyond the sheer loveliness of the "dress of the evening" (which I felt and am convinced was the prettiest one there) was the realness of you as a person. Your personhood is coming along nicely. As a father, I revel in your intellectual and spiritual maturation.

During the new year of 1983 I want to make a pledge to you. I am going to pray in a most special way for you each day. I am specifically going to claim from God for you: 1) **Abounding creativity**; 2) **Innovation** in your studies and career discoveries; 3) **Sizzle** ("It's not the steak that attracts the diner; it's the sizzle.") Sizzle is that "extra something" that turns ordinary into extraordinary!; 4) **Professionalism** in your emerging role as a productive society member—and your upcoming senior year of college; 5) **Management** of your time, talents, creativity, innovation, sizzle, and professionalism. (Management will help you place new ideas, new outlooks, and new skills into a quality productivity); and, of course, 6) **I wish you LOVE**—for yourself, your friends, and for that special one guy He is preparing for you.

Blest wishes my dear,
Your Dad

My dad did meet the man I married and for whom he had prayed, my wonderful husband, David McSweeney. Yet only months before my wedding, my dad passed away from a massive heart attack while on a business trip in Paris. I wish that we could have had one final dance.

On those days when I need a hug from heaven, I unfold the worn and smudged letter from my desk drawer. After almost thirty years, my dad's gentle words still guide me with his great life lessons. Each time I slip the letter back into the desk, I smile through my tears and remember to "sizzle."

DAD'S MARK
BILL HYBELS

Recently my brother and I spent a lunch hour discussing the mark our dad left on our lives. Dad wasn't a perfect man, but he was authentically masculine. He loved God deeply and knew how to be firm yet compassionate.

Dan and I reminisced about the times we had sailed with him on Lake Michigan. We remembered violent storms with fifty-mile-an-hour winds. All the other sailors would dash for the harbor, but Dad would smile from ear to ear and say, "Let's head out farther!"

We talked about the tough business decisions we had seen him make. We winced when we remembered his firm hand of discipline that blocked our rebellious streaks. We never doubted it. Dad was strong and stalwart, tough, and thoroughly masculine.

Yet for twenty-five years he spent nearly every Sunday afternoon standing in front of a hundred mentally retarded women at the state mental hospital. Gently and patiently he led them in a song service. Few of them could even sing, but he didn't care. He knew it made them feel loved. Afterward he stood by the door while each of those disheveled, broken women planted kisses on his cheek. As little guys, Dan and I had the unspeakable privilege of watching our six-foot-three, two-hundred-twenty-pound, thoroughly masculine dad treat these forgotten women with the gentleness that marked us.

If you're a dad, what kind of mark are you leaving on your children, especially your sons? Do you realize that your little boys are watching you like hawks? They're trying to figure out what maleness is all about, and you're their model. I hope they see you in a deep, uncompromising love for God. I hope they see both toughness and tenderness. If they do, then you have served them well; they will be forever grateful.

A PRESENT FOR PAPA

NORENE JONES

Dear Papa,

It's Father's Day. Another year and once again I stand before you with my pitifully inadequate gift. Your other children and all our offspring have already paid you homage, and now it is my turn.

The house I have known since childhood is noisy and crowded. Grandchildren run through the rooms, and from the kitchen come familiar sounds, familiar odors. The meal today will be basted carefully as always with love, turned with gentleness, and served with laughter—all the things we were raised on daily in your house.

In the midst of the family gaiety you sit smiling and happy in your favorite chair. The chair is part of you and so much like you—friendly, comfortable, and dependable.

I watch you enjoying your day, surrounded by those you love. Your hands, holding my four-year-old, are veined and creased with time. Those hands. They pointed out the Big Dipper to me. They showed me how to bait a hook, plant a bulb, and pull an oar. Now I watch them teaching my child to tie a bow.

Your eyes now wear spectacles, but the glass cannot contain the merriment, the enthusiasm for life behind its frames—the same contagious enthusiasm you tried to teach me. How many dawns did we wait and marvel at a sunrise together? How many days did we put to bed? Glowing sunsets settling into an azure lake.

Your hearing is not as keen as it was thirty years ago, but I'll bet you can still hear the breeze come up through the old cottonwood in the front yard. "Listen," you said to me over and over. "Just listen." And I learned the cry of the hawk, the call of a dove, the rhythm of the rain.

You taught me to taste. "If you don't try new things, you'll miss half of life's pleasures," you said. I still remember my first wild blackberry. You gave it to me right off the bush.

And wading in an icy stream to drink water from a tin cup. Did anything ever taste so good? And tiny tart apples from our own tree—the tree you planted for us. You gave me so much for so many years, and what did I give to you? A sport shirt you'll probably never wear. You'll act surprised and pleased, and then it will join the boxes of ties and pajamas and cigars surrounding you.

"Happy Father's Day," I say at last, and stoop to kiss your white head. But, oh Papa, I wish I had a wild blackberry to give you, or a fresh lake bluegill. Or maybe a drink of spring water from a tin cup.

Your grateful daughter.

Next Summer—on the Ice!

Laurele Riipa

I grew up in a small, rainy lumbering town in western Washington State during the 1950s and the 1960s. Days seemed to move in slow motion, school years were endless, and summers seemed even longer. Dreaming up creative ways to pass long days was a challenge after hours of reading, coloring books, paper dolls, or running around the neighborhood. Television was about the same age that I was and, as I recall, offered little programming for kids other than the magical Mickey Mouse Club and the fabulous Saturday morning cartoon lineup, which I watched religiously with my older and younger brothers (but not the oldest, my sister, who was above such things by then). Our household was a traditional one with Mom at home and Dad working most of the time— two jobs, in fact—as a carpenter during the day and the local movie projectionist several nights a week. We just didn't get to spend a great deal of time with him—alone or otherwise. To make matters worse, four of us kids were all vying for his attention—a most difficult situation.

Daddy was a quiet, gentle, steady sort of guy. As a girl, I was surprised to hear stories about rash, spontaneous behavior during his youth. It seems that he and a bunch of his college pals went "AWOL" in an old jalopy and headed for the 1933 Chicago World's Fair for some R & R. When his father found out about this recklessness, he was not happy with his only son. In those early Depression years, pocket money wasn't too easy to come by even if he was working his way through school, but I thought it was wildly romantic of him.

I often relate to Daddy in the summertime since those balmy evenings bring back vivid memories of the smell of our newly cut lawn and raking, then filling the wheel barrow with the grass. To finish, Daddy would roll that old wheelbarrow a few blocks away, cross over the railroad tracks, and dump the cuttings into the tall willows and cattails near the bay. Going with Daddy to the tracks became a favorite ritual even when I had to share him with one or two of my brothers. (I won't even begin to tell you how enthralled I was with a trip to the local dump.) On other evenings, I would casually suggest (with the support of my younger brother) that we go to the Oriole, an old-fashioned soda fountain and café. When hints turned into straight out asking and then became begging, you knew it was not going to happen, particularly when Dad teased with the reply, "Sure we'll go—next summer on the ice!" But when we caught him in *just* the right mood, it was a heavenly long walk to town where you knew comic books and a root beer float awaited. The Oriole was a gathering place for many. I think Daddy liked the casual conversation with friends also out for a little socializing. By the time we were on our way home, I was always painfully sleepy and surprised by how much farther away home seemed. Even so, walking in the darkness, hand in hand with Daddy was the final treat of the evening.

I don't recall him talking all that much or ever having any kind of memorable discussions during these special times spent together. He was a man who may have been introspective, but clearly never felt the need to discuss matters. For me, it was just important to be with him. Years later in my teens when most kids wouldn't be caught dead hanging around either parent, I still managed some special time with him. Now I'm surprised that I got the unique privilege over my brothers to help him change the oil and grease the car. Oh rapture! I thought this was just the coolest thing. I still loved that precious one-on-one time together even though it was under the car, inching around on a gravel driveway. Personally, I think I made a pretty darn good assistant. At least then, when I'd ask him if I could help, he never said, "Sure. Next summer—on the ice!"

THE VOICE OF A GOOD MAN

KRISTIN ANDRESS

I love the sound of my dad's voice. We now live two thousand miles apart, though we talk at least two times a week. Distance is not a factor. The older we grow, the closer we get. Dad is retired now, so there is more time to talk. From the weather to politics to TV shows, we always find things to talk about. There has not always been a flow between us, but now we are never without it.

My parents divorced when I was six, but he was a very involved dad. He attended every event of my brothers' and mine, and like clockwork he picked us up for weekends, which were filled with boating, fishing, and sports. We have a cabin on the Illinois River, and in the wee hours we would launch the old, green John Boat and check trout lines. Later, we would rev up the speed boat and Dad liked to see who we could find to race. Often we would stop and float and Dad allowed us to take 'dips' by jumping overboard. We did not have all of the fancy boat toys at first, so Dad was creative. He would tie on the boat to a fallen tree and have us ride it behind the boat or he would drill a hole in a door, add a rope, toss it in the water, and tell us to jump on. We would line up and hold on for dear life as he pulled us around. Finally, he bought a zip sled and he would drive in fast circles to see if he could bounce us off. We were not coddled, and we had a blast. Often, as a little girl, I curled up under his feet on the floorboard to nap. The buzz of a boat and the chop of the hull on the water still have the power to make me serene. We would end the day with hotdogs or hamburgers on the grill, and popcorn while watching a football game.

Dad has a gift for having fun. He taught me to enjoy the ride. He taught me many things about which he may be unaware. He did not retire until his early seventies. He valued his work and appreciated being valued. He taught me the power of doing a job very well, and humbly. He is known as the fertilizer king of the Midwest, which he shrugs off as just doing his job. Dad has stayed busy in retirement, and informs me about mowing yards, replacing air conditioners, and visiting my brother at his archery shop. He taught me to continue to contribute and grow.

I witnessed Dad's grief and his recovery over the abrupt death of one of my brothers. He keeps the memories alive and honors living life. Today, we can laugh over Kent's antics and all of the chaos he instigated when we were kids. Dad taught me to survive the tough stuff in life.

My stepmom and I were sitting on a beach in Bermuda a few years ago watching Dad splash in the water, and bask in the sunshine, and she said, "Your dad is a good man." Yes, he is. I wonder if he knows it. There are so many things I love about the good in him.

I love it when Dad laughs. His entire face lights up and he has the most beautiful, twinkling blue eyes. I love when Dad tells stories of his past. They usually involve some kind of mischief. I love when Dad gets belligerent about the decisions of a politician and weighs in with his opinion of what should be done. I love when Dad gives me stuffed animals, even if I'm in my forties.

I love that Dad is my biggest cheerleader. He tells everyone what I am up to in the world, and I am moved when I hear the pride in his words. He makes me feel good about myself.

My favorite words from his voice are "It's my Baby Boo!" Dad said, as soon as he heard me when I was born, he knew I was his girl. And…I have been ever since.

A LULLABY

DEANNA ALLEN

When I was young my dad would work from eight to five every weekday. I'm only seventeen now, so it wasn't so long ago. When he got home, he was tired from packing and moving boxes and figuring out where things went in the warehouse. After dinner he relaxed by sitting in his recliner and watching TV with my mom.

When it was time for me to go to bed I wasn't nearly as tired as he was, so to help me fall asleep my dad would get out of his recliner, take a break from watching his old, cowboy, shoot-em-up shows, pick me up, and take me on a walk. I remember being so excited when we left I barely heard the swinging screen door slam shut behind us.

Sometimes he asked what I did that day and I would tell him about the wonderful picture I fingerpainted or the cookies I helped my mom bake. When I got too sleepy to continue talking or to pay much attention to anything, he would sing to me. He didn't always sing exactly on key, but his voice was really deep and it sounded perfect. My favorite song was "Away in a Manger." I don't know why, but he would sing it to me even in the middle of spring.

I remember he held me just a little bit tighter when we walked by the barking dogs, all the while still singing. I would drift off to sleep feeling his warm breath on my neck as my head rested on his shoulder. I never really remembered getting back to our little white house, but I always woke up the next morning, warm in my bed.

$\mathcal{D}$AD'S TIMEPIECE
ISABEL CHAMP WOLSELEY

"Dad, I'll level the clock after a while. It's not ticking evenly. I think it's sitting crooked on the shelf."

"That so? Hadn't noticed."

Dad replaced the key and closed the lace-patterned glass door. He wound it each Monday morning before leaving the house to do his chores. That clock had been a wedding gift to my parents fifty-five years before. It was supposed to be an eight-day timepiece, but it slowed each weekend and ever since I could remember, winding it had always meant the start of a new week for the three of us.

A still-sleepy sun filtered through the screen door, momentarily silhouetting Dad. I saw he carried the pan of potato peelings and eggshells left from preparation of our farm breakfast; I heard his worn boots count each step from the porch, then trace the dusty path to the chicken yard.

"Come peeps! Come clucks!" Fat biddies and babies raced to the gate anticipating tidbits he had for them. I smiled to myself, thinking, *Recycling is a recent concept and here Dad has done it all his life. I wonder how many times those eggshells have gone through those hens?*

Mom and I chatted over coffee in the front room. We reminisced about how the two of them had held me in those same rockers when I was a child. They'd been "Mama and Daddy" back then. And even on recent occasions I'd used those endearments when I had deep concern that I felt only they could understand.

It was comforting to be back in the white clapboard home. Other visits had been such short ones when I was rearing my own family in Oregon. Probably my husband was at that very moment flowing along in Portland's traffic on his way to work. It seemed so quiet and peaceful—in spite of the rooster's crow and the bawling calf. Between the barn and the chicken house was the windmill, which did double duty as a weather vane. Beyond it was a wheat field.

"I'd forgotten how the wheat waves—just like the ocean," I said. "Kansas really is 'The land of the south wind.' Even the trees lean somewhat to the north."

Mom went outside with a basket of clothes to hang on the line. She ignored the dryer except in wet weather. "The wind whips out the wrinkles and the clothes smell good," she said.

The wind played crack-the-whip with the sheets on the line as I turned my attention to the clock. It struck nine healthy bongs as I tore several bits of cardboard to tuck under its scrolled sides. Aligning it was no problem, especially with help of the level I found in the cellar toolbox. Its faded red paint was peeling, but the still-accurate bubbles helped me level the clock on the slanted shelf.

And yet…it seemed the clock still ticked unevenly. I sat again in the yet-warm rocker, trying to think why. As I looked around the room, I became aware of its unevenness. Not only was the clock shelf awry, but so were the floors, the walls, the doorjambs. In fact, the whole house slanted somewhat toward the north—just like the trees.

I began to think how the old farm home had not resisted, but had serenely submitted to the elements. Even the clock had adjusted its tick and conformed.

Dad was bent too. He didn't let the south wind's drought or hailstorms break him—he conformed. "Look up. There's a purpose for everything," he'd say and then start in again without complaint. And, yes, his gait was uneven, like the clock's; yet, he was a pillar to me and Mom. Remembering his resiliency to trouble had helped me rear his grandsons. And though his back was bowed, he could "look you straight in the eye"—his favorite expression of honesty. His life was peaceful and free of ulcers or worries.

Suddenly I heard Mom screaming my name. I dashed to a window and saw Dad on the ground. His left fist clutched his chest; his right protected the pan emptied of potato peelings and now filled with freshly laid eggs. Frantically, I dialed the operator for an ambulance.

That day and others at the hospital passed endlessly for Mom and me. Through the Intensive Care Unit door, I saw Dad, pale beneath his oxygen tent, laced with tubes and instruments. Thank goodness, his heart still ticked! The beeper of the cardiac monitor confirmed it.

Just one person was allowed in with him for five minutes each hour. The other fifty-five, we waited in the corridor. Only occasionally did Mom allow me to take a turn with Dad. I brought her trays from the cafeteria, but she scarcely touched them. Her comfort was not in food, but in sitting by Dad, watching his face and unknowingly tracing and smoothing the veins on his weather-browned hand.

Daily I drove to the quiet farmhouse to take care of their chores. Odd how I'd always relied upon Mom and Dad. Now they needed me…but I seemed to have no strength to give in return.

I scattered feed to the chickens and held a bucket of milk for the calf to drink. I thought of Mom and how her eyes left Dad's only to look beseechingly at nurses or me. It had been a week. Usually seventy-two hours was long enough to determine life or death in such cases. Dad had said, "There's a purpose for everything." Was he right?

While the calf butted his artificial feeder, I remembered another of Dad's encouragements: "Look up." Then from somewhere in my recollection came a verse from Scripture, "Call upon Me in the day of trouble; I will deliver thee…."

I closed my eyes. "Lord, this is the day of trouble—that I know. How You'll bring deliverance—that I don't know. But those are Your words."

Leaving the contented calf with his mouth and nostrils covered with milk foam, I was anxious to get back to Dad. An expectancy I didn't understand surged as I turned the time-worn skeleton key to lock the back door, then drove out the hedgerowed lane toward town.

When I reached Dad's room, Mom was wearily starting in for her hourly five-minute vigil. I patted her gently back down into the chair in the corridor. "Let me go in this time, Mama." After a long, wondering look, she nodded.

Dad was still unmoving, still uncomprehending. I stroked his hand and silently said, "Lord, Mom needs him. So do I. But he's so weak—he'll never make it on his own. Only You can make him strong and well again."

Nothing new happened. The oscilloscope's needle continued its irregular tracing. The cardiac monitor beeped. Dad's breathing stayed humpy and broken.

As I thought about my prayer, I was embarrassed. It was so…well, childish. *But I am His child*, I thought. And so is Dad. In that grim situation, I relaxed.

Then imperceptibly Dad's breathing seemed to strengthen. It was like his clock—which still ticked unevenly, yet stronger, when wound. As the hours passed, his face showed a flicker of consciousness and by evening Mom and I were able softly and briefly to talk to him.

"Everything's all right out at the home place, Dad," I assured him. "I took care of the chickens. The calf is fine too. And Dad…Daddy…I wound the clock this morning."

"That's so?" he whispered. "That starts a new week."

I knew then that I knew Dad was going to make it. And he did.

A MILLION MILLION
DEBI STACK

"Daddy, how much did I cost?"

Perched on my parents' bedroom cedar chest, I listened to their casual talk about budgets and paychecks—talk as relevant back in 1967 as it is today. My then six-year-old mind concluded, wrongly, that my family was poor.

Dad stood at his dresser, looking at bills. He wore faded jeans, an undershirt, and white canvas shoes stained grass-green from mowing our lawn. Mom folded laundry on the bed, making even towers of sun-dried clothes. I spotted my new shorts sets and thought about day camp.

Their money talk continued, and Dad joined me on the cedar chest. I plucked the springy metal watchband on Dad's tan wrist, thinking that the white skin underneath reminded me of a fish belly. Just as I started to ask him to "make a muscle" so I could try pushing his flexed biceps down, a thought hit me like icy water from a garden hose: *Dad had to pay for me.*

While the story of my birth ranked as a bedtime favorite, I had never considered hospital bills…or the countless meals I'd eaten…or the price of summer clothes.

"Daddy," I interrupted again, "how much did I cost?"

"Oh, let's see." He sighed in distraction and placed his watch on the safety of his dresser. "About a million dollars."

A light went out inside of me. *A million dollars.* Because of me, Dad worked two jobs. Because of me, he drove an old car, ate lunch at home, and had his dress shoes resoled—again.

With my eyes and chin down, I inched off the cedar chest and shuffled into the kitchen. From a shelf, I took my granny-shaped bank, which held every penny I owned—seven dollars even. And not seven dollars in assorted change, but seven, cool shiny silver dollars. One for every birthday, and one for the day I was born.

The bank's rubber plug surrendered, and the coins poured into my damp hands. I had often played with these coins in secret, jostling them in a small drawstring bag in my roles as gypsy or runaway princess. They had always been put back in the bank, though, and I felt secure pleasure in just knowing they were there. But that day, the "clink" of returning each coin sounded hollow.

If the topic had changed when I returned to my parents' bedroom, I didn't notice. Tugging on Dad's shirt, I held out my first payment on a million dollars.

"Here," I sniffed. "Maybe this will help pay for me."

"What?" Dad's confused look matched my own. Didn't he remember what he'd said? Didn't the sight of me remind him of how much I cost?

My tear-filled eyes, which I couldn't seem to take away from the bank, finally made sense to him.

Dad knelt down and pulled me close. "You didn't cost a million dollars, but you're worth a *million*-million dollars. And if that's what I'd have to pay for you, I'd do it. Now dry those eyes and put your bank away."

At the time, I felt some relief that Dad didn't have a million-dollar debt, but more relief that I hadn't lost my silver dollars.

Today, I often pull out this memory, turn it over, and feel the warm, satisfied weight of it in my heart. Back then, no price could be put on my worth to my dad. No price can be put on his worth to me now.

Thanks, Dad. I love you too.

THE COMPANION

BETH HACKETT

Have you ever thought about why you do some of the things you do? Is it all simple routine or does it have meaning? Your morning cup of coffee, for example. Do you drink it for the taste or because you need a jolt? For me it's neither.

Don't get me wrong, I love coffee. The smell of freshly ground beans, the silky sweet taste, the warmth of the mug in my hands—these are good reasons to drink coffee, but I drink it because of my dad.

I was an only child. Mom said I was plenty; Dad said I was perfect. He worked hard to support us: twelve-hour shifts with thirteen days on and only one day off, because overtime paid the bills. He left early in the morning, long before Mom and I were awake; he came home exhausted and slept until it was time to do it all over again. It was hard on him because he had so little time with us. It was hard on us too.

We all found ways to compensate. Mom would pack his lunch and take one bite of his sandwich, so he would smile when it was time to eat. I would put my favorite toy in his lunch box so he had something to play with at work.

Dad's special time for me was morning coffee. He would get up at 4:00 AM, start the coffee brewing, and get ready for work. When the pot was ready, he would come into my room and wake me up. I would sit at the kitchen table as he poured two cups of coffee. His was always black. Mine was barely brown, full of milk and sugar, sweet to the taste. Dad would tell me about his day and ask about mine. When the cups were empty, he would tuck me back into bed and kiss me good night before heading out to work. It was our special time together, and we never missed it.

When I moved away from home, we talked on the phone every day. Now our special time was cooking dinner together. He cooked for Mom, I cooked for my husband. We never missed it.

He died in 1995, and I still miss him. Every morning I make a pot of coffee and sit at the kitchen table. My coffee is still just barely brown, full of milk and sugar, sweet to the taste. When I raise my mug to my lips and drink that first sweet sip, I see my dad sitting across from me, a smile on his face and a cup of coffee in his hands. Saying good-bye does not torment me, because I know Dad will be back tomorrow. My cup of coffee is never routine. It's always special. I'm having coffee with my dad.

MY FATHER'S CHRISTMAS

CRYSTAL WARD KENT

My father has that look so often associated with the outdoors—skin tanned from wind and sun, weathered hands (he never wears gloves), and the kind of frame that always seems most at home in hunting jackets, ball caps, and boots. To look at him, one would not see a weaver of holiday beauty. That role would seem to belong to artsy women in floral shops, not to a crusty Mainer, now in his midseventies.

But from my dad's fingers come wreaths of balsam, yew, boxwood, and holly. He fashions garlands and ropes, creates centerpieces and corsages. My father learned his craft as a teenager, taught by his dad, who had learned from his. There was no formal training involved, just one generation showing another the ways of the evergreens, and how to change a bit of greenery into something magical.

His greens come from our land, a modest acreage in the small town of Eliot. When my parents first married, my father started a nursery as a way to supplement their income. They were living in a trailer, both working multiple jobs as they saved for a house. The sturdy little trees thrived and grew, and over time were sold. Today, few of the original plantings remain, and my father is retired. But there is enough greenery for traditions to carry on.

As the days shorten, my father's greenhouse becomes an island of light and warmth, adrift in the darkness and cold. The greenhouse smells like summer soil spiked with balsam. Only one part of the workbench is covered with cuttings—my father makes everything fresh and will not cut until he is ready to create. An old Styrofoam wreath frame, veteran of countless holiday seasons, lies ready, waiting to be transformed. To one side, decorations are piled in a jumble of color. Glistening balls of red, silver, and gold, crimson holly berries, snowy white reindeer of plastic and wood (very old). These are his tools of magic. Bows hang from the greenhouse rafters, parading in red, white, gold, and burgundy. These are the classic colors, the classic looks, my father says. These are tradition. Other colors—plums, mustards, blues—they are fads; they come and go. But red bows and holly berries, gold balls and prancing reindeer, these spell Christmas. These are what people request year after year.

My father's fingers fly as he works. Clip and stick, clip and stick. Swiftly he cuts the holly into gradually longer lengths, all the while inserting it into the wreath frame. He steadily layers the wreath, building it from the outside in. Meticulously, he checks for gaps, holes or wayward strands. My father's wreaths are unique; they do not have big holes in the center. They are round masses of greenery and color. Satisfied, he begins decorating. No two will look the same, so he chooses his decor with care. Now, the bow, then the finishing touches, a spritz of snow for the evergreens, or shine for the holly. The wreath is briefly scrutinized, then hung in the greenhouse until delivery.

Sometimes there is a special request, but most recipients of my father's wreaths trust his sense of color and theme. They wait each year to be surprised at the morsel of holiday magic he has woven. And his handiwork never fails to delight. The wreaths make their way to the town hall, the library, the SPCA for a charity auction, church fairs, an historic home, and to old friends and neighbors. Sometimes the recipients are those facing an especially difficult Christmas—a parent is ill, a divorce occurred, a son is overseas. The circle of decorated greenery is especially meaningful to them, a sign that someone cares.

My dad enjoys delivering the wreaths himself. Like Santa Claus in a pickup truck he makes his rounds. He carefully unloads the wreath, then bounds into the house or office with a whiff of cold air and evergreen trailing behind him. Seeing the smiles and hearing the exclamations are his reward. A cup of coffee, a bit of a chat, and he's off to his next stop. This ritual has been part of his holidays for decades.

I have seen him at work hundreds of times, yet it suddenly strikes me that I am not just watching a wreath come to life, but the holidays themselves. For each wreath is crafted with caring, with personal regard for what the recipient might like. Each wreath carries with it a message of tradition and family, of taking time to create something special. My father would never admit this, but love is woven into each garland and wreath. For he gives all of his creations away. And as they are hung on a door or wall, they carry the true spirit of Christmas with them.

FATHER KNOWS BEST

WHEN I WAS A BOY OF FOURTEEN, MY
FATHER WAS SO IGNORANT I COULD HARDLY
STAND TO HAVE THE OLD MAN AROUND.
BUT WHEN I GOT TO BE TWENTY-ONE, I WAS
ASTONISHED AT HOW MUCH HE HAD LEARNED
IN SEVEN YEARS.

~MARK TWAIN

MY FATHER'S FLAG

KATHRYN SLATTERY

Maybe you've noticed: Flag Day usually comes up on the calendar right around Father's Day. My dad would like that.

When I was a nine-year-old girl in Medfield, Massachusetts, the highlight of the year was marching with my Brownie troop in the town's Memorial Day parade.

Even today, I vividly remember marching behind the high school band and the DAR ladies in their vintage bustles and gaily feathered hats. We smiled and cheered and waved tiny American flags distributed by the Kiwanis Club men.

The parade route ended at our town's cemetery. There I met up with Dad, and together we listened to a long speech delivered by the town's oldest World War I veteran. I quickly grew bored and my thoughts drifted away like a dandelion puff on the soft summer breeze. But not Dad. He stood tall and alert, and cocked his head to catch every word.

My father had served in the Naval Air Transport Service during World War II, and as the soldiers at the cemetery gave their twenty-one-gun salute and the trumpeter played "Taps," his eyes never left the flag.

Looking back, I can't help but wonder: *Who knew what lost friends my father was mourning?*

As I grew older, I admit that Dad's patriotism sometimes embarrassed me. *A lot.* I wanted to hide when he lustily bellowed every last word of "The Star Spangled Banner" at high school football games. Not only that. Sometimes he would get all misty-eyed. I just couldn't understand what made my father tear up at the sight of the flag.

One day I asked him.

"The flag stands for everything we believe in," he said. "Freedom. Justice. Sacrifice."

Those were the values my father lived his life by.

When Dad died, a large flag draped his casket, courtesy of U.S. Veterans Affairs.

"You take it," my mother said to me after the funeral, handing me the folded triangle of red, white, and blue. "Dad would want you to have it. One day you can pass it on to your children."

I took the flag home and put it away for safekeeping on the top shelf of a closet. That was more than thirty years ago. Over the years I have taken it out and hung it more than I ever thought I would—and not on just the obvious holidays. I put it out on Veterans Day, and on September 11, and, of course, on June 14—Flag Day.

This year I think I'll keep it up for Father's Day to remind myself of those enduring values my dad talked about: Freedom. Justice. Sacrifice. They would never survive without getting passed along—by everyday patriots like my father.

A SHARING OF WONDER

ARTHUR GORDON

Many summers ago a small boy lived in a tall house by the sea. The house had a tremendous peaked roof made of weathered shingles that towered above all the surrounding cottages. In this roof, near the top, was a trapdoor that could be reached only by a ladder propped up on the attic floor. Children used to play in the attic sometimes, but no one ever climbed up to the trapdoor. It was too high and forbidding.

One sunny day, however, when the boy's father was storing some boxes in the attic, he glanced up at the underside of the great roof. "Must be quite a view from up there," he said to his son. "Why don't we take a look?"

The boy felt his heart lurch with excitement and a touch of fear, but his father was already testing the shaky ladder. "Up you go," he said. "I'll be right behind you."

Up they went through the mysterious darkness, each step a terror and a delight. Up through the tiny sunbeams lancing through the cracks, up until the boy could smell the ancient heat-soaked shingles, up until the trapdoor, sealed with cobwebs, touched the top of his head. His father unhooked a latch, slid the trapdoor back…and a whole new universe burst upon his dazzled eyes.

There lay the sea—but what a sea! Gigantic, limitless, blazing with splintered sunlight, it curved away to infinity, dwarfing the land, rivaling the sky. Below him, queerly inverted, were the tops of trees and—even more unimaginable—the backs of gulls in flight. The familiar path through the dunes was a mere thread where heat waves shimmered; far away a shrunken river with toy boats coiled into the sea. All this he saw at a glance from the protective circle of his father's arm, and the impact of such newness, of such violently expanded horizons, was so great that from that moment the world of his childhood was somehow altered. It was stretched, it was different, it was never quite the same again.

Decades have passed since then; most of the minor trials and triumphs of childhood have faded from my mind. But I remember that moment on the roof as if it had happened yesterday. And I think of it sometimes when the day set aside as Father's Day comes round, because it seems to me that the real Father's Day is not this sentimentalized, overcommercialized occasion at all. The real Father's Day is the day that exists only in memory, in the mind of some happy child or nostalgic adult, the magical day when—just for a moment or perhaps simply by accident—a chord was struck, a spark jumped the gap between generations, a relationship was suddenly achieved so warm, so intense, that it was caught and held in the meshes of the mind, impervious to time.

My father has been dead for many years now, but he left so many Father's days behind him that he doesn't seem to have gone very far. Whenever I want to feel close to him, all I have to do is choose one from the assortment in my mind labeled "The time we..." Some are little-boy memories like the day on the roof, some are teenage recollections, some no doubt would seem trivial to anyone else, but all have the same quality: a sense of exploration, a discovery of newness, a sharing of wonder.

There was the time we went to see a captured German U-boat that our Navy had brought into the harbor. We climbed down into the maze of machinery smelling coldly of oil and war and claustrophobia and death. Another visitor asked my father bitterly if he did not consider the German sailors murderers who struck without warning from the depths of the sea. I remember how he shook his head, saying that they, too, were brave men caught like their adversaries in the iron trap of war. The answer did not please his questioner, but somehow brought relief and pride to me, as if a sudden test had been met and mastered.

Or the time we explored a cave, and at one point far underground snapped off our flashlights and sat there in darkness and silence so profound that it was like being in the void before the beginning of time. After a while Father said, in a whisper, "Listen! You can hear the mountain breathing!" And such is the power of suggestion that I did seem to hear, in the ringing silence, a tremendous rhythm that haunts me to this day.

Did my father deliberately set out to manufacture Father's Days for his children? I doubt it. In the episodes I remember so vividly I don't think he was primarily seeking to instruct or inspire or enlighten us. He was satisfying his own curiosity— and letting us in on his discoveries. He was indulging his own sense of wonder—and letting us share it.

This is the stuff of which real Father's Days—and Mother's Days also—are made.

Sometimes, when the formula works, the parents may not even know it. But sometimes you do know, and when this happens there is no satisfaction in the world quite like it.

Not long ago our family visited one of those marine establishments where trained porpoises—and in this case a small whale—put on a marvelous show. I was so fascinated by the whale that I lingered after the performance to ask the trainer how it was captured, what it was fed, and so on. He was an obliging fellow who not only answered the questions but summoned the whale herself to the side of the pool. We patted her back, smooth and hard and gleaming like wet black rubber. This evidently pleased her, for suddenly she raised her great barrel of a head out of the water, rested it on the coping and gazed with friendly, reddish eyes at our eight-year-old daughter, who was nearest.

"Apparently," I said, "she wants to rub noses with you."

Our daughter looked both interested and aghast.

"Go ahead," the trainer said good-naturedly. "She won't mind."

There was an electric pause, then the briefest of damp contacts, then both participants hastily withdrew. And that seemed to be the end of it, until bedtime that night. Then, staring pensively at the ceiling, my daughter said, "Do you think any other third-grader in the whole wide world ever rubbed noses with a whale?"

"No," I said, "I'm pretty sure you're the only one."

She gave a deep, contented sigh, went to sleep, and hasn't mentioned it since. But thirty years from now, when her nose tingles, or when she touches wet black rubber, or sometimes for no reason at all, maybe…just maybe…she will remember.

SET FREE
PTOLEMY TOMPKINS

My father was never much for rules. Anything that smacked of restriction—of "no you can't"—drove him crazy.

The more obvious reasons for this were not hard to find. At a very early age, my father's parents had sent him off to a superstrict boarding school: the kind of place where the schoolmasters were mean, the food was terrible, and every minute of every day was defined by what you couldn't do.

Those schools left their mark on my father. The memory of those mean schoolmasters made him fearful and suspicious of authority figures, from traffic cops to librarians. The memory of countless meals of moldy potatoes and horse meat turned him into the fussiest of eaters, always complaining that the food in front of him wasn't quite fresh enough. And the memory of all those rules—all those endless don'ts— made him virtually obsessed with the idea of freedom. He determined that his own life was to have as few rules in it as possible. Preferably none.

Is life possible without rules? Not if you listen to the teachings of the world's religious traditions—and especially not if you listen to the Bible. Thou shalt; thou shalt not. Those two phrases sum up the essential biblical attitude that without rules, the world is ordered by chaos. They also sum up the mind-set that my father most detested. Rules might indeed make the world an orderly place, but if so, then it was better to live in chaos than to be subjected to them.

As it happened, chaos was precisely what my father's no-rules lifestyle ended up producing. As a child, I accepted the dramas and disasters that came along with having a freedom-obsessed father, but by the time I was in my early thirties my patience had run out. In 1999—the same year I came to work at Guideposts—my father and I stopped speaking.

Not that I was entirely happy with this situation. Each time I'd write a story that made use of some lesson my father had taught me—which happened surprisingly often—I'd find myself wondering what he'd think of it if he saw it. But then I'd remember some offense my father had committed—one of the countless hurtful or destructive situations that he had created through his relentless insistence on living outside all the ordinary rules of human conduct—and I'd shake free of my nostalgia. I'd washed my hands of my father, and I was the better for it.

In the summer of 2006, I got a call from my nephew, who was visiting my father at his West Virginia farmhouse.

"How's he doing?" I asked.

"Good," my nephew answered. "But he looks way older and weaker than the last time I saw him. He wishes you guys could get past your differences."

Those words were all I needed. I sent my father an e-mail; a message popped back into my in-box almost instantly, and within a couple of days we were conversing as if just a week or two had passed since we last had spoken.

That fall, for the first time in nearly a decade, I drove down to visit. I found my father in his book-crammed, hopelessly cluttered study, stretched out on the daybed where he used to take naps in between spells of work.

My nephew was right. He was older, and he looked weaker. But at the same time, he was very clearly the same person he'd always been. He smiled, reached out, and grasped my hand, and within a few minutes was lecturing me at full force on the latest political conspiracies he'd uncovered.

Along with politics, one topic at the forefront of my father's mind that weekend was his health. He'd been suffering from prostate cancer for years, but had successfully managed to keep it under control. Some recent tests, however, indicated that it might have returned.

"I'm investigating some really mind-blowing new alternative therapies," my father said with that trademark nothing's impossible tone I knew so well. Giving in to cancer, after all, would have gone against my father's whole philosophy. Not even death would get in the way of his quest for freedom.

Throughout the rest of the fall I kept in touch with my father by phone and e-mail, and told him I'd come back to visit as soon as I could. One Friday after an extra-busy week at work, I called to check in and noticed that he sounded a little weaker than usual.

"If you're really feeling bad I can come down now," I said.

"No, no," my father said. "Come when it's best for you. I'm doing fine."

Just two days later, my father's friend and nurse Rebecca called. "If you want to see your dad," she said, "you'd better come right away."

By the time I got there that evening, my father was barely conscious.

"Ptolly's here," my sister Robin, who'd arrived ahead of me, said into my father's ear when I came in.

"I know," my father said, without opening his eyes. "I can feel him."

For the next three days, my family, Rebecca, and I took turns sitting by my father as he drifted in and out of consciousness. I picked up a generous supply of Red Bull at the local market and offered to take the all-night shifts.

Those last long evenings were some of the strangest and most significant I'd ever spent with my father. There were moments, as he lay there with his eyes closed, mumbling softly to himself, when I got the uncanny sense that, beneath those closed lids, my father was looking at something: something I couldn't see, but that seemed to be filling him with an extraordinary amount of joy. Maybe, I thought, he was getting his first glimpse of that landscape where freedom—real freedom—is truly available at last.

On one of these evening vigils I happened to spy, up on the shelves of the study and partially obscured by a stack of books, the hull of a child's wooden sailboat. Rebecca, I figured, had dug it up from the junk out in the barn and placed it there for decoration. I stared idly at the boat for a few moments before I recognized it.

My father had given the boat to me many years before, during one of our summers in New Hampshire. Taking it down from the shelf, I saw that it was scratched, dusty, and missing its mast, its sails, and the delicate set of strings and pulleys that it had been outfitted with when my father had first presented it to me. But it was unmistakably the same boat. Looking at its black enamel hull and the miniature metal fittings set carefully into the smooth wooden planking of its decks, I remembered the protective feeling that the boat's jewel-like perfection had instantly inspired when my father had first gave it to me. The last thing I'd wanted to do was put it in the water.

Yet at the same time, I did want to put it in. There was a large pond near our house with a sandy beach perfect for launching my new craft. But directly across from the beach there was an overgrown swampy area. Brambly plants grew right down to the shore, making approach from land just as difficult as from the water. What if my new boat ended up over there in that boggy wasteland? I might never be able to get it back.

"Why aren't you putting your boat in the water?" my father had asked as I crouched at the pond's sandy edge, fiddling with its sails.

"Because," I'd answered, "If I do, I might not get it back."

"That," my father had said, "is precisely why you should put the boat in the water right away. Set its sails properly and set it free. It'll come back to you if it wants to."

Set it free. Despite all the protests my father had made to me about the God of the Bible over the years, he and that God had some things—some very important things—in common. Though He might appear as a bossy tyrant, the God of the Bible is really every bit as ardent a believer in freedom as my father was. That's why, throughout both the Old and the New Testaments, He is forever allowing His children to fail, and fail, and fail again…and forgiving them each and every time they do. It's also why He forgives them not only when they fail to live up to His commandments, but even when they turn their backs on Him completely. For it is only by allowing humans to act as they will that He does justice to that uniquely human ability to choose one's actions independently, with no help from Him whatsoever: an ability that sets human beings above even the angels in God's sight.

My father died at 6:00 AM on Wednesday, January 24, 2006, at the age of eighty-nine, at the end of my final evening vigil with him and just a few short months after we'd forgiven each other our differences and come together again as father and son. Just like that sailboat my father had given me so long ago, I'd sailed away from him. But in the end, free as all of us ultimately are to choose what is best, I had found my way back.

DRIVING LESSONS
CHARLES SWINDOLL

I remember when I first earned my license to drive. I was about sixteen, as I recall. I'd been driving off and on for three years (scary thought, isn't it?). My father had been with me most of the time during my learning experiences, calmly sitting alongside me in the front seat, giving me tips, helping me know what to do. My mother usually wasn't in on those excursions because she spent more of her time biting her nails (and screaming) than she did advising. My father was a little more easygoing. Loud noises and screeching brakes didn't bother him nearly as much. My grandfather was the best of all. When I would drive his car, I would hit things...*Boom!* He'd say stuff like, "Just keep on going, Bud. I can buy more fenders, but I can't buy more grandsons. You're learning." What a great old gentleman. After three years of all that nonsense, I finally earned my license.

I'll never forget the day I came in, flashed my newly acquired permit, and said, "Dad, look!" He exclaimed, "Whoa! Look at this. You got your license. Good for you!" Holding the keys to his car, he tossed them in my direction and smiled, "Tell you what, Son…you can have the car for two hours, all on your own." Only four words, but how wonderful: "All on your own."

I thanked him, danced out to the garage, opened the car door, and shoved the key into the ignition. My pulse rate must have shot up to 180 as I backed out of the driveway and roared off. While cruising along "all on my own," I began to think wild stuff, like *This car can probably do one hundred miles an hour. I could go to Galveston and back twice in two hours if I averaged one hundred miles an hour. I can fly down the Gulf freeway and even run a few lights. After all, nobody's here to say, "Don't!"* We're talking dangerous, crazy thoughts! But you know what? I didn't do any of them. I don't believe I drove above the speed limit. In fact, I distinctly remember turning into the driveway early…didn't even stay away the full two hours. Amazing, huh? I had my dad's car all to myself with a full gas tank in a context of total privacy and freedom, but I didn't go wild. Why? My relationship with my dad and my granddad was so strong that I couldn't, even though I had a license and nobody was in the car to restrain me. Over a period of time there had developed a sense of trust, a deep love relationship.

After tossing me the keys, my dad didn't rush out and tape a sign on the dashboard of the car, "Don't you dare drive beyond the speed limit" or "Cops are all around the city, and they'll catch you, boy, so don't even think about taking a risk." He simply smiled and said, "Here are the keys, Son, enjoy it." What a demonstration of grace and faith. And did I ever enjoy it!

FULL CIRCLE
JANNA L. GRABER

From my bedroom I heard the sharp flip of a light switch, and then the thud of my father's footsteps in the hallway. I turned over in my bed and groaned, knowing exactly what his next words would be.

"It's seven o'clock. Time to wake up!" came his cheery voice.

I pulled the pillow over my head. "Can't I sleep in a little bit this morning?" I complained. After all, I thought, I was eighteen years old now.

"We've got chores to do," my dad replied in a voice that said I should know better. "Everyone's ready for breakfast already."

I grumbled as I got ready. *Why couldn't I live in a normal family?* I thought.

By the time I got downstairs, my family was already seated around the long oak table in our kitchen. My seven younger brothers and sisters, ranging from age sixteen down to age one, sat poised to pounce on the food as soon as the blessing was said.

With eight children, eight of them adopted, my family was not the normal suburban household. To top it off, we lived in a farmhouse on a small acreage that was surrounded by the Denver suburbs. The idea of doing chores—feeding livestock, cleaning barns, and gardening—was foreign to my city friends. While they slept late or watched cartoons on Saturday mornings, I was doing chores with my family—something I was beginning to dislike.

Breakfast had been devoured by the time I finally turned to my dad. "What's the job today?" I asked, making it clear I thought I should still be asleep in bed.

"The orchard," he replied. "It needs watering and weeding. If we work together, it'll be done in an hour."

The "orchard" was nothing more than twenty knee-high saplings. Two of my sisters pulled the hoses out to water, while Mom and Dad got down on their knees to weed. I grabbed a hose too, and halfheartedly pointed water on the trees struggling to survive in the dry Colorado soil.

"No, you've got to let it soak in," my father said as he walked over to inspect my work. "Keep the hose on them longer."

My frustration was hard to hide. "Why do we have to water these dumb sticks anyway? They'll never amount to anything!"

Dad looked at me evenly, as if considering a proper response. "These 'dumb sticks' will someday grow into beautiful trees. Your mom and I want a nice home for our family. It's a dream we have." He paused, and I saw his eyes scan our home, then turn to rest on my siblings. "Most dreams take hard work and time," he continued. "You need to keep that in mind."

With that, he went back to work, leaving me to consider his words. I looked at my family. Mom was helping two of my brothers pull weeds around the raspberry bushes, while a sister looked over the two youngest who were playing in the grass. My dad had chosen the hardest job of planting another young sapling in the hard clay earth.

I saw sweat on his brow as he toiled under the searing sun. Why, I wondered, did he do it? Why did he work so hard for us?

"Hey, Dad," my brother Philip called, "come look at my work!"

My dad walked over to Philip, who, at twelve, was struggling to fix a broken fence. Philip's work was clumsy, and bent nails protruded from the uneven slats he had replaced. But he beamed with pride as he showed off his handiwork.

I snickered. Couldn't Philip see that the job would need to be redone?

My dad's response surprised me. "Good job!" he said. "You went to it and got it done!"

The scene made me wonder. It would have been easier if Dad had done the job himself. What benefit was there for my brother to bungle through the work?

And why didn't we move into a house that required less upkeep? Did my parents enjoy all this work, or did they have another motive?

The home we lived in now looked nothing like when we had bought it. Built during the Depression, the whole farmhouse had consisted of two rooms and a tiny added-on kitchen. But my parents had seen the home's potential. They spent the next few years remodeling and landscaping. When the house got too small, they built on—three times—until the once-small farmhouse was a lovely home just right for raising eight children. I had never really thought about all my parents had done for us—until now.

I was quiet as I went back to my work, wondering about my parents and what they were trying to teach us.

Years have flown by since that day in the orchard, but I've thought a lot about my father's words. "Most dreams take hard work and time," he had said. "You need to keep that in mind."

Those sentiments echoed in my mind through college and a new career. In fact, my father's words and example have become so engrained that sometimes they begin to slip out.

When I purchased my first home, it was clear the place needed some work. The bare landscape needed attention, and I purchased dozens of flowers, bushes, and tiny trees.

A few days later, I invited my parents for a visit, and proudly showed them my purchases.

"Let's put them in," my mom said, as she headed to the garage for a shovel.

We eagerly planted and got to work. I took the shovel, and had begun to dig a hole when I stopped. There was something missing.

I ran inside the house, and found my two daughters who were watching a video with a friend.

"Come on outside and help," I called. "We can plant these trees together."

A surprised look came over their faces as I showed them how to hold the trees as I planted them.

"But those don't look like trees," my oldest exclaimed. "Why do we have to do this?"

My answer came without thinking, "If we do it together, the job goes much faster. Besides, they may not look like much now," I told her, "but with a little work and time, they'll grow into something beautiful."

Then, out of the corner of my eye, I saw my father grin.

THE TOOLBOX

JOSHUA HARRIS

Recently my dad and my younger brother Joel attended a birthday party for Stephen Taylor, one of Joel's best friends. It was a very special occasion. Stephen was turning thirteen, and his dad wanted to make Stephen's entrance into young adulthood memorable. Nice presents wouldn't suffice; Stephen's dad wanted to impart wisdom. To accomplish this he asked fathers to accompany their sons to the party and to bring a special gift—a tool that served them in their specific lines of work.

Each father gave his tool to Stephen along with its accompanying "life lessons" for the "toolbox" of principles Stephen would carry into life. The tools were as unique as the men who used them. My dad gave Stephen a quality writing pen and explained that a pen not only served him when he wrote his ideas but also represented his word when he signed an agreement.

During the gift giving, a father who was a professional homebuilder handed Stephen a small box. "Inside that box is the tool I use most," he said. Stephen opened it and found a nail puller.

"My nail puller, simple as it might seem," the father explained, "is one of the most important tools I have." This father told the story of how once, while in the middle of building a wall, he discovered that it was crooked. Instead of halting the construction and undoing a little work to fix the wall, he decided to proceed, hoping that the problem would go away as he continued to build. However, the problem only worsened. Eventually, at a great loss of materials and time, he had to tear down the nearly completed wall and totally rebuild it.

"Stephen," the father said gravely, "times will come in life when you'll realize you've made a mistake. At that moment, you have two choices: You can swallow your pride and 'pull a few nails,' or you can continue your course, hoping the problem will go away. Most of the time the problem will only get worse. I'm giving you this tool to remind you of this principle: When you realize you've made a mistake, the best thing you can do is tear it down and start over."

TAKEN FOR GRANTED

DONNA PENNINGTON

It's strange looking back on my relationship with my dad, because for the first thirty years of my life we didn't have much of one.

No, we weren't separated by divorce, long hours at work or even a grudge lingering from my not-so-pleasant adolescence. Over the years I'd developed a vague composite of my father—a tall, shy man who worked very hard.

I just never really paid him any mind. He was a fixture that I took for granted.

Then nine years ago, when I was pregnant in my second trimester and bleeding, my dad showed up to offer his help. I was surprised. Sure, in the past he'd given me financial aid, fatherly advice, and fixed broken appliances, but money, words, and tools weren't going to prevent a possible miscarriage.

Still, every day he came. He took me grocery shopping, did the heavy chores of cleaning, and, undeniably, maintained my household.

At first I felt awkward having my retired dad around on a daily basis. I even felt guilty at times. I didn't know how to relate to this calm, quiet gentleman because at the time that's all he was to me—a nice, helpful man.

But somewhere between folding laundry together and watching *The Oprah Winfrey Show*, we started talking. It seemed silly that it took a talk show's calamity to break the ice between us. Yet soon we were voicing our opinions on everything from politics to child rearing. Then things got more personal, and we started swapping life stories.

My dad became a remarkable man who had a fascinating history—and a new granddaughter.

After the baby, Dad continued coming over and helping out. Our projects began extending beyond household chores, and he taught me how to hold a hammer "like a man." We built furniture, then a shed. To this day, he arrives religiously at my door every other week to help me get ready for Girl Scout meetings in my garage.

My friends find it amusing that my dad is still helping out even though my two girls have started school full-time, but they don't understand. It's not just about the work anymore. Working together broadens our understanding of each other. I doubt the issues of race, religion, and morality would have come up during a brief lunch at the mall. So you're more likely to find my dad and me complaining about the inflated price of nails inside a hardware store than having a polite conversation over a hamburger. He is my best friend, after all, and that involves more than talk of the weather.

Knowing him is to understand what makes a man noble.

When he reads this, he'll probably laugh and wonder what the heck I'm talking about, but I know him now and that's an honor I almost lost.

So, to anyone searching for a true friend, I recommend starting with the person you may have taken most for granted.

LOVING-KINDNESS

MY FATHER USED TO PLAY WITH MY BROTHER
AND ME IN THE YARD. MOTHER WOULD
COME OUT AND SAY, "YOU'RE TEARING UP
THE GRASS." "WE'RE NOT RAISING GRASS,"
DAD WOULD REPLY. "WE'RE RAISING BOYS."

~HARMON KILLEBREW

ᵔATHER'S FISHING ROD
JOSHUA KLEIN

It so happens that my father likes to tell stories, often of no particular relevance except for the fact that he likes them. While I grew up under this sort of tutelage, it took me until I was into early manhood to recognize the value of this ritual.

Besides being a storyteller, my father is also a fisherman of sorts, inasmuch as he loves to fish. There was one story that he used to tell every time he went fishing, often with me sitting blackly in the car beside him, having been threatened (I felt) into going on another fishing expedition. The story would occur when we were packing up the car, on the way to the fishing site and while we unloaded the car. He would tell it again as we rowed the boat out to the middle of the lake, and as we tied knots and untangled lines. That story was the tale of my father's fishing rod.

When my father became a young man, his father took him to the local store and, with great care and much father-and-son love, bought him a fishing rod. I could never tell what was so special about the rod, but my father always handled it as though it were either very expensive or highly explosive. He would relate to me over and over again, each time his eyes misting over and his face beaming in a sort of private joy, how he had measured his height and caught his first fish with it. And if I did not change the subject soon, he would go on to relate the tale of each and every fish he had caught with it thereafter. But it was made clear to me at a young age that when I was old enough I could use the rod, and as it was rather outdated and my father had other rods better suited to his advanced frame, I ended up using it most of the time.

Like most teenagers, I was usually difficult to deal with. My parents have loved me, and always will love me, truly and with all their hearts. But I think it was around the age of thirteen that I really tested the lengths to which they would go to continue loving me rather than simply breaking my neck. That year we went on a family vacation around the San Juan Islands, traveling in a boat my father had rented. It was incredibly beautiful country, and even my teenage bitterness and cynicism faded after a few late-evening sunsets and early-morning sunrises. I had even managed to get on fairly well with the family, and had stormed out of the cabin and onto the boat top only a few times the whole trip.

Near the end of the trip I was allowed to sleep up top. That meant an evening of relative privacy for me, a precious commodity. It also meant being able to fall asleep with the stars as my roof and the gentle sounds of the ocean as my lullaby. Not that I would have admitted it then, but the idea rather appealed to me. I even submitted graciously to the idea of fishing for a spell before turning in, laying the rod beside me as I read a favorite book by lantern light.

The moment was a perfect instant in all things: the sunset's last glimmers just disappearing on the horizon, the stars coming out in the velvet sky above. And on a little boat was a little boy, just getting up to unroll his sleeping bag and go to sleep...

And then it happened: Plunk. That was all, just a gentle plopping sound as the world around me began to spin and I turned to see my father's fishing rod, his pride and joy, sink beneath the inky waves.

There were frantic moments of running about, splashing with the net and the eventual discovery of what happened. Then came the anguished cries of my father, tears, and yelling and screaming. Soon I found myself huddling in the bow, amid the extra life jackets and ropes and other sundries. It was as far as I could get from the rest of the world, and I cried and cried there. I prayed for the first time since I had been allowed to not go to church, and I prayed for everything from forgiveness to death.

The whole time I was concerned most not by fear of my father, nor by the thought of punishment, but by something more important: the dreadful fact that I had hurt my dad. In those few short minutes, which stretched into hours, as the yelling and stomping above me faded into the gentle sounds of a man deeply hurt, I realized that I loved my dad. And that no matter what, no matter what happened, I always would.

There was no way to pay back what that rod represented. I could never take him back to the days when his father was alive and escort them to the town store. All those boring times I had listened halfheartedly to the story about the fishing rod suddenly seemed immeasurably precious, moments to be treasured for all time.

Eventually my mother asked me to come out, and the family spoke for a long while. We spoke of grief, and my father told me that he didn't hate me for what had happened and that it was okay. He told me that he still loved me and that he always would. And we cried together as a whole family—me, my sister, my mom and my dad. And finally we all went to bed and fell into a deep, sad sleep.

The next morning my father and I got up quietly and went to pull up the crab pots. We smiled a little at each other and didn't say anything, because we didn't have to. The sun was high and the waves were blue, and even though something horrible had happened it was okay, because we both loved each other and that was enough.

As I set a crab pot down with a thunk on my side of the boat, I turned to hear a gentle laugh coming out of my father. His crab pot was beside him on the deck, and he was leaning over the edge of the boat, carefully pulling on something. A fishing line was tangled in the crab pot, and he was slowly trying to retrieve whatever was at the other end.

Then in the quiet morning air, my father and I gently pulled his fishing rod up from the bottom of the ocean, and cried and laughed together, until my mother and sister woke up to join us.

LIKE FATHER, LIKE DAD

LISA ZEHNDER MAAS

I'm not shoplifting, I'm exchanging, I rationalized, as I left the department store dressing room wearing a new pair of jeans. But when I walked out into the mall, a woman grabbed my arm. "Security," she said. "Come with me." In the office I cried while a guard called my dad.

He picked me up and we drove in silence. Dad was a Lutheran pastor, and the disciplinarian in the family. Ashamed, I kept my face lowered. He pulled into the driveway and stopped the car. Then he turned to me. I wanted to tell him how sorry I was, but I couldn't even look him in the eye.

"We're never going to mention this again," he said, and he hugged me hard. I couldn't understand why he had forgiven me so easily.

At church the next day, Dad gave a familiar sermon; I had heard him preach about God's grace many times. But never before had I understood so well.

$\mathcal{F}$ORGETTING FATHER'S DAY
RICK HAMLIN

Father's Day and not a word from Timothy—not even a quick "Happy Father's Day!" at the breakfast table. It was not like him to forget. It made me nostalgic for Father's days of the past when both boys were around. I could remember magical days at the ball field, cheering them on. I could recall picnic suppers in the park and handmade cards and clay creations. But not this year: William had a summer job in California, and in the afternoon we would be taking Timothy upstate to his job as a camp counselor. The day would be spent behind the wheel of a car. After the long drive, Carol and I would come home, eat dinner, and I'd watch Tim's and my favorite TV show all by myself.

That's all right, I told myself. The boys are busy doing other things—as it should be at their ages.

William called on the cell phone as we were driving back from camp. I was touched. But Timothy hadn't mentioned anything, even when I hugged him good-bye. The house seemed deathly quiet. I washed dishes, brushed my teeth, and went to watch TV. I was just about to plop myself down on the sofa when I noticed a bright turquoise envelope on my usual spot. "Papa," Timothy had written on the card inside, "I hope it's a good episode tonight, even without me there. Happy Father's Day!"

When someone loves you, they know you well...and know just where to find you.

NOT ALL VALENTINES COME IN ENVELOPES

ROBIN JONES GUNN

As a teenager, I worked as a waitress at a Coco's restaurant, in Southern California. Although California nights are supposed to be warm, on this particular February night the brisk wind shrieked through the front door. Around nine o'clock things slowed down and that's when I started feeling sorry for myself. You see, all my friends had gone to the movies, but I had to work until closing.

I didn't pay much attention to the man who entered the restaurant. A flurry of leaves followed him in. The sound of the wailing wind fell silent as the door shut itself. I busied myself making more coffee. Suddenly the hostess grabbed my arm. "This is really creepy," she whispered, "but there's a man with a white moustache over there who said he wouldn't eat here unless you were his waitress."

I swallowed hard, "Is he a weirdo?"

"See for yourself," she said.

We carefully peered through the decorative foliage at the mysterious man in the corner. Slowly he lowered his menu, revealing thick, white hair, silver-blue eyes, and a wide grin beneath his white moustache. He lifted his hand and waved.

"That's no weirdo!" I said. "That's my dad!"

"You mean he came to see you at work?" The hostess balked. "That's pretty strange, if you ask me."

I didn't think it was very strange. I thought it was kind of neat. But I didn't let Dad know that. Poor Dad! I acted so nonchalant, rattling off the soup of the day and scribbling down his order before anyone could see him squeeze my elbow and say, "Thanks, honey."

But I want you to know something—I never forgot that night. His being there said a thousand things to me. As he silently watched me clear tables and refill coffee cups, I could hear his unspoken words bouncing off the walls: "I'm here. I support you. I'm proud of you. You're doing a great job. Keep up the good work. You're my girl. I love you." It was the best valentine I received that year.

STICK SHIFT
CLARK COTHERN

The day I drove a white, 1960 Ford pickup truck to high school, I had my eye on a cute little flute player who sat in the front row during band. Jeanie was fourteen and claimed to have "vast experience" driving a stick shift. I figured one way to impress a fourteen-year-old girl would be to let her drive "my" truck around the school parking lot. Jeanie became very excited about the possibility. I became very excited that she had become very excited. What a wonderful way to flood sunshine on a blossoming relationship.

Only two problems existed with this arrangement. First, "my" truck actually belonged to my dad. Second, the only thing "vast" about the girl's experience with stick shifts was the size of her imagination. Her actual logged *experience* with a stick shift, it turned out, amounted to one quick drive in somebody's VW Bug.

After my hasty explanation of which pedal did what, she followed my instructions and pushed in the clutch, extending her short left leg as far as it would go. With her toes trembling, she held that pedal down.

With her other foot, she gently pressed on the gas pedal.

The old truck roared to life as she turned the key. As I had explained, she began slowly lifting up on the clutch with her left foot while at the same time slowly depressing the gas pedal with her right foot.

That's when the plan began to unravel.

Her footwork became a bit erratic when the clutch engaged and the truck lurched forward. She tried to cram her foot back down on the clutch pedal but forgot about her right foot, which was jammed down as hard as she could push…onto the accelerator.

Sitting in the middle of the wide seat, I watched little sections of the nearby shop-class building whiz by in the rearview mirror. I felt like a rodeo cowboy riding his first bucking bronco as the truck jerked forward in wild, untamed motions.

Trying to remain calm, I yelled, "It's okay!" Who was I kidding? With nothing to hold on to, I was lurching back and forth like wet jeans in an unbalanced spin cycle.

"Just push down on the clutch and let off the gas," I hollered above the noise of the engine, which was revving and dying in time to the jerking motions of the truck.

"Which one's the clutch?" she screamed back. I guess my lesson hadn't sunk in.

"The one on the left," I said.

"Is what?" she asked. "Which one is the brake?"

We really didn't have time for this conversation to be taking place since we were quickly running out of parking lot. Just about the time I thought to help her by grabbing the stick shift and yanking it into neutral, I noticed the chain-link fence looming dangerously close to our left just ahead.

The fence wasn't what bothered me so much. It was the faculty parking lot filled with cars just *beyond* the fence that really got my heart racing.

Suddenly, before I had a chance to turn the key to "off" or to grab the steering wheel and turn it toward open space, I heard the sickening sound of metal against metal. Nice, straight, shiny-aluminum poles began bending like pipe cleaners as the Ford-pickup-turned-tank mowed down a healthy section of newly installed fence.

Finally, for lack of gas and momentum, the old truck stalled, and silence filled the cab. I noticed my friend's cute little legs trembling as she stood straight up on both pedals, with her knuckles white and locked onto the steering wheel.

"Well," I said, breathing for the first time in several agonizing seconds, "that wasn't so bad, for a first try."

She crawled over my lap onto the passenger side of the truck while I surveyed the damage from the window. I couldn't believe what I was looking at. The bumper of the heavy old truck was resting less than twelve inches away from the bumper of the vice principal's Buick Regal.

My heart finished the bossa nova and returned to regular rhythm again, and I decided to own up to the experience. I backed the truck into an actual parking space, thanked my young friend for a lovely time, and excused myself to the vice principal's office.

Maryvale High School in Phoenix was quite large at the time since Trevor Brown High was still under construction to our west. So, with five thousand kids to handle, our principal, David Goodson, only dealt with major issues like riots and gun control. The vice principal, aka "No Mercy" Miller, was the guy who got to hear all the really good stories...like the one I told him.

I took full responsibility for my actions and for driving the truck into the fence, feeling a bit unsettled by the wide, silly grin on his face the whole time.

When I finished my tale of woe, Mr. Miller said, "Tell you what you do. Call this number," and he handed me a business card. On it was the name and phone number of a fence company.

"They just installed the fence you ran into...*yesterday*."

My knees grew weak. It was at that very moment I realized just how fortunate I had been. If that fence hadn't been there to stop our forward progress—like a cable stopping jets on an aircraft carrier—we would have nailed Mr. M's Buick but good!

He continued, "Tell the owner what happened, and see if he'll let you pay for the damages out of your own pocket. Since this happened on private property, we won't have to call the police for an accident report."

Sigh. Ah, at that moment I could have almost kissed that man. Almost. The VP could have given me what I really deserved—or worse—but instead, he gently helped me learn my lesson and take responsibility for my actions. He remained absolutely calm through the entire ordeal.

I called the name on the card, and a very kind man answered, "Oh yeah, heard about that little incident." I didn't know if he was loud because he was shouting over machinery noise or because he always talked like that, "I'm a little surprised to hear from you," he shouted. "One of my installers called me with the details. Says he was able to bend back three of the four posts you knocked down. The fourth one snapped like a toothpick. Why don't you come down here to my office and pay me…oh, say, ten bucks for the pipe, and we'll be back in business."

All the way down to his office I was repeating, "Thank You, God. Oh, thank You, thank You, thank You!"

With that taken care of, I faced the most difficult part of this trial. I still had to break the news to my dad.

I parked the truck as far up in the driveway as I could, with the left front fender facing away from the house. When Dad arrived home from work, I caught him as he was stepping out of the car, so I could set the right mood.

"Hey, Dad, how was work?" I acted really friendly. Maybe a tad too friendly.

"Just fine, Son. What's up?" He must have been able to tell by the way I was shifting my weight from side to side that I was a little hyped. That and the fact that my voice was up to an E-flat.

"Well, Dad, you'll never guess what happened today at school. The funniest thing." I laughed, mostly out of pure nervous energy but also hoping he would catch it and laugh with me, at least just a little.

Using the most animated and humorous expressions I could muster, I explained in detail, from start to finish, the entire episode to my father, including the fact that the vice principal had worn that silly grin on his face the whole time I was telling him my story. Then I said, "Kinda like that one you've got on your face right now, Dad!" and I laughed some more.

He sighed, chuckled, shook his head from side to side, and then put his hand on my shoulder and said, "Let's take a look at the truck."

I tried to find enough saliva in my mouth to swallow as we walked around to the damaged fender and surveyed the scratches. They weren't that bad, considering what it'd been through that day. Those old trucks were really built. He looked at the damage, sighed one more time, and then said, "You know what happened to me and one of my brothers when I was about your age?"

Suddenly I was able to swallow. I had heard his sermons before, but I figured being preached at was better than some other forms of punishment he might have devised. I acted really interested.

He said, "Your uncle and I found an old truck that belonged to our dad, your grandfather. We decided to surprise him by getting the truck down the hill, into the barn, and back into working order."

(This was getting interesting. Better than most of the sermons I'd heard before.)

"Well, it wasn't until we got the old truck rolling downhill that we made a very important discovery. There were no brakes. In this instance it wasn't a chain-link fence that stopped the truck. It was a four-inch by four-inch fence post."

I caught myself gawking just a bit, so I closed my mouth, which had opened as Dad revealed this compelling truth about his boyhood. Not as fearful as I was before his story, I awaited sentencing.

Dad said, "I suppose that if you sand this area, first with a coarse grit and then with the fine one, we could probably match that color pretty well with a store-bought spray and just touch it up a little. This is an old truck, after all."

It had been a hat-trick day for gentleness. Three times in one day I had not been yelled at. Not once.

First the vice principal, then the man at the fence place, and now my dad. I almost couldn't believe this was happening. I followed Dad's advice, and in no time at all we had the old truck back in nearly good-as-used shape. The whole day had been a terrific learning experience for me: telling the truth to the vice principal, paying for the fence, helping with the bodywork on the truck, and all the while absorbing an even more valuable lesson in the process.

I learned that day about gentleness and about teaching lessons to sons who make mistakes. Dad's message sank in deep because he combined strength with gentleness. The gentleness softened the shell around my heart and allowed the arrow of truth to pierce right into its target.

LESSONS FROM A WALLET
BRUCE McIVER

When I arrived back home in North Carolina after Dad's fatal heart attack, I found his well-worn wallet. In it were some identification cards and six crisp fifty-dollar bills. There were no credit cards.

"Mother," I asked, "what are all these new bills doing in Dad's wallet?"

"He knew you and your family were planning to come home in a couple of weeks for your vacation, and he wanted to have some cash on hand so you wouldn't have to spend any of your money while you were here."

I smiled through tears. I should have known, for that was the way Dad was, and it's taken me most of my life to figure it out.

George Sylvester McIver was born in a log cabin near Bear Creek, North Carolina. He and Mother left the farm shortly after they were married and made the journey seven miles west to the thriving small town of Siler City. Dad went to work in a furniture factory and lived by the factory whistle for forty-five years. He never made a lot of money by today's standards, but money was not an issue that was discussed around our house.

Except once.

"Ollie," he said to my mother when he came home from work, "I stopped at the grocery story and picked up the items you said we needed. This sack of groceries cost two dollars and sixty-eight cents! We've simply got to cut back on what we buy."

As a seven-year-old boy, I watched and listened in disbelief. Wow! Two dollars and sixty-eight cents—enough to buy just about anything a fellow could ever want.

Looking back, there were times when Dad made two dollars a day in wages, but we had plenty—and more. We lived in a white bungalow that he and Mother had helped build with their own hands. Late at night she would hold the kerosene lamp and Dad would hammer together the finishing touches of the ceiling. We grew our vegetables, milked the cow, churned the butter, raised and killed two hogs a year, made preserves out of blackberries and watermelon rinds, and had fried chicken straight from the backyard anytime we desired. My clothing, if inexpensive, was warm and comfortable; and my own mattress, filled with straw or feathers, provided all the luxury a growing boy could hope for as he lay down to sleep.

There was usually a nickel for chocolate candy at Rose's Five-and-Ten-Cents Store, or a double-dip cone of ice cream at Ed Kidd's Sandwich Shop. A dime could always be found somewhere for a western picture show at the Elder Theater on Saturday afternoon, and Dad always came through with fifteen cents for a Friday night basketball game. Sometimes he gave me a quarter, which meant I could have a cold soft drink and some popcorn.

And more.

When I was nine years old, I was stricken with osteomyelitis, an infection and inflammation of the bone. Three major surgeries were performed on my hip at Duke Medical Center where I was a patient for sixty-nine days. The cost of the surgeries and the hospitalization were never mentioned in my presence. Several years later, after I had my own family and became aware of medical expenses, I asked Dad how in the world he managed all the bills while I was sick.

"Oh, it wasn't that bad," he replied. "We managed without any difficulty." And, with those words, the conversation about the costs of my surgeries and hospitalization ended.

Years later, after he died and after I found his wallet, Mother and I were driving around Siler City, basking in memories and reliving warm experiences. I turned a corner, drove up a street, and passed a house that looked familiar.

"Mother, didn't Dad used to own that house?"

"Yes, he owned it once."

And then, almost without thinking, she added, "I believe that's the house he sold to pay your hospital bills."

Tears welled up in my eyes—tears of gratitude. It took forty-two years to get the answer to my question. And I should have known it all along, for that's the way Dad lived...and died.

The crisp fifty-dollar bills found in his wallet said it all.

He knew we were coming home.

A FATHER'S BLESSING

MORGAN CRYAR

Many a morning as a child I stumbled though the darkness to our family's truck, fell back to sleep, then was awakened by the sound of the truck sputtering to a halt in the Louisiana woods. I can remember, even when I was too young to dress myself, climbing out of that truck alongside my dad—the most important person in my life at the time—and stepping into the gray, early morning light to hunt squirrels or deer.

One morning ten years ago I was once again headed for the woods to hunt with Dad. But this time I was grown, with a family of my own. I had been touring for months and had promised to make a trip from our home in Nashville, Tennessee, to the swamps outside of Lake Charles, Louisiana, where I had grown up. Though I didn't know it, this would be no ordinary morning. It was the morning that I would find out that Dad approved. This morning he would give me his blessing.

When we got into Dad's old truck and he turned the ignition key, music began to pour from a cassette in the tape deck. I knew the music well and was surprised to hear it in Dad's truck. It was my most recent recording, blaring into the morning stillness! I couldn't help myself. I said, "I didn't know you even had this. Do you listen to it?"

His answer amazed me. "It's the only thing I listen to." I glanced around, and sure enough, it was the only cassette in his truck. I was dumbstruck! He said, "This is my favorite," referring to the song playing at the time. I let his words sink in as he turned down the volume to match the morning.

We drove in silence down the road toward the hunting spot, and I wondered at what had just happened. It seems now like such a small thing—a few spoken words. But there seemed to be something different in the air. I sat taller in my seat. I looked at my dad out of the corner of my eye and thought back to two turning points in our relationship.

One turning point happened while I was in college. I remembered having it dawn on me that I had never heard my dad say that he loved me. I knew that he did, but I couldn't remember having heard him say so. That was something my dad just didn't do. For some reason it became important to me that I hear those words from his own lips. I knew, however, that he would never initiate it. So that summer, as I drove home from college, I determined to "force his hand" by telling him *first* that I loved him. Then he'd have to say it back. It would be simple. Just three little words. I anticipated a glorious new openness once I had come home and said, "I love you, Dad," and then he would respond.

But simple is not always easy. The first day came and went, and I thought, "*I have to tell him tomorrow!*" The next day came and went. Then the next, and the next. Then twelve weeks passed, and it was the last day of my summer break. I was frustrated at not having said those three little words to my dad.

My small, beat-up car was packed and sitting on the gravel driveway. I promised myself that I would not start the engine until the deed was done. To someone with an emotionally open relationship with his own father, this may all seem a bit silly, but to me it was serious business. My palms were wet and my throat was dry. My knees grew weak as departure time came.

It had been a good summer visit. There was a general sadness in the house because I was headed back to school across the state. Finally I could wait no longer. I hugged my mom, my brother, and my sister good-bye, and went back to find my dad.

I walked up to him, looked him in the eyes and said, "I love you, Dad."

He smiled a half smile, put his arms around me and said what I needed to hear: "I love you too, Son." It seemed as though a thousand volts of electricity were in the air as we hugged each other (another thing that hasn't happened since I was a small child). It was such a little thing, but it changed everything!

From that point on, all of our conversations were signed off with: "I love you, Dad." "I love you too, Son." It became commonplace to embrace when we greeted each other and when we parted. As plain as it sounds, it resulted in a new sweetness between my dad and me. The memory of it came back to me in the truck that morning on the way to the woods.

The other turning point came after college. I remembered what I had learned at a seminar about clearing my conscience with those whom I had wronged. This was entirely new to me—admitting guilt and receiving forgiveness from those I had offended.

Part of the process was to ask God to show me anyone and everyone with whom I needed to clear my conscience. Sure enough, at the top of the list was Dad.

So I sat down with my dad and started first with the worst things that I had done. I proceeded from there to the least serious offenses. I confessed everything that I knew had hurt him, even from my childhood. Then I simply asked, "Dad, will you forgive me?"

Just as I had expected, Dad was embarrassed and tried to shrug it off: "Aw, it's all right, Son."

I said, "It will mean a lot to me if you will forgive me."

He looked right at me and said, "It has already been forgiven."

That was his way of saying that he had not held a grudge. And once again, everything changed. From that moment Dad treated me with new respect. I hadn't anticipated it, but he also began to treat me like an adult—like a friend.

In the stillness of the morning, on the way to the woods, these things floated through my memory, and I rested in my dad's approval of my calling, my work, my music.

I had no way of knowing just how precious his blessing would become to me. One short week later, after my family and I had driven back to Nashville, I received the telephone call from my brother Tommy, telling me that Dad had walked onto the porch and had died of a heart attack. He had been young and healthy—only forty-nine years old. It was my darkest day.

Though my family and I tasted intense grief, I still had much for which to be grateful. I had enjoyed thirty years with my dad—some of them as his friend. He had given me a strong enough start that I knew I could meet the challenge of rearing my own children, including my son who was born on Father's Day six years later.

Even though my dad is gone, in the wee hours of that morning on the way to the woods, he had given me something of great value to pass along—a father's blessing.

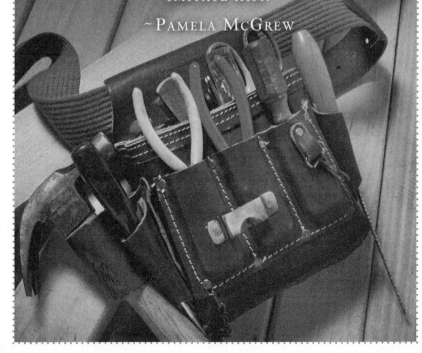

Role Model

MY FATHER NEVER TALKED TO ME ABOUT
HOW TO TREAT PEOPLE. EVERY ACT OF
KINDNESS I HAVE EVER SHOWN ANOTHER
PERSON WAS BECAUSE I WAS TRYING TO
IMITATE HIM.

~PAMELA MCGREW

A New Pair of Shoes

Willie B. Raborn

Keeping up seemed so important when I was a teenager. Back in 1963, if you weren't wearing penny loafers you'd just as soon go around in your bare feet. I was thirteen years old and had worked hard to keep up with my peers. There was only one problem that year: I had bought oxfords—but penny loafers were in. I asked my dad for help.

"I need some money for penny loafers," I told him one afternoon at the shop where he worked as a car mechanic.

"Willie," he said in apparent shock, "the shoes you have on aren't a month old yet! Why do you need new ones?"

"Everybody's wearing penny loafers, Dad."

"That might be, Son, but that doesn't make it any easier for me to pay for them." Dad's salary was small and seldom covered more than rent and groceries.

"Dad, I look like a fool wearing these things."

Dad looked at me for a full minute before he answered. "Tell you what," he said. "Wear those shoes one more day. Look at every pair of shoes you see at school. If you can tell me that you are worse off than the other kids, I'll take part of your mom's grocery money for you to buy new shoes."

Triumphantly, I went to school the next morning, knowing that it would be the last day I'd have to appear out of style. I did what Dad said, but I had no intention of telling him the results.

Brown shoes, black ones, stained white tennis shoes—they all seemed to have a personality of their own. By noon I'd seen shoes that were scuffed beyond recognition, torn shoes of the likes I'd never had to wear, and shoes with holes in them that made me wonder how the kids wearing them ever kept their feet dry on rainy days. And then there were those gleaming black penny loafers with the horseshoe taps that demanded attention when they clicked in the halls.

When school was out, I rushed to the shop where Dad worked, knowing I'd return to school the following Monday as part of the "in" crowd. Every now and then I dragged my heels on the pavement, imagining how the taps would sound when they were in place later that night.

The shop was quiet when I arrived. Only an occasional clank of metal could be heard as Dad worked under a 1956 Chevy. Even the smell of old motor oil pleased me that day. One man sat alone in the shop waiting for Dad to finish with his car.

"Mr. Alva," I asked the man who was waiting for his car, "is Dad almost finished?"

"Can't ever tell, Will. You know your dad. He's working on the linkage on the transmission, but if he sees anything else wrong, he'll fix that too."

I walked to the car to wait. All I could see were Dad's legs from the knees down. I stood there fingering the taillight of the Chevy as I stared at Dad's feet.

His shoes were old and black, the kind mechanics and service-station attendants wear. The left one had two stitches of baling wire where the soles had long since separated. The laces had been spliced on both shoes. Neither one had a heel, only small, bent nails where the heel had been pulled off. Dad had bent them to keep them from pushing through to his feet.

"That you back there, boy?" Dad asked, coming out from under the car.

"Yes, sir," I said.

"You do what I told you today?"

"Yes, sir."

"Well, what do you want to do?" He looked as though he might know what my answer would be.

"I still want the penny loafers." I forced myself not to look at his shoes.

"I have to take your mom grocery shopping as soon as I get off work. Why don't you go ahead now and get the shoes?"

Dad handed me ten dollars and fished in his pocket for change to pay the three-percent sales tax. I took the money and went to the store two blocks down the street.

I stopped in front of the store window to see if the shoes were still on sale. They were, for $9.95, but I wouldn't have enough money left to buy the necessary taps. I decided to wait until I got home and ask Mom for the money. I couldn't ask Dad for more right then.

When I thought of Dad, his old shoes flashed through my mind. I could see the mended soles, the spliced laces, the bent nails in the heels. He had worn the leather off his shoes working for us, his family. Surely his feet got cold on those nights when he got calls to go across town to start someone's car, yet he never complained. I thought of clients like Mr. Alva, whom Dad was always doing something extra for, even if they never asked. I thought of Dad going without things he needed so I could have things I wanted, and the gleam on the loafers in the window started to dull.

What if Dad had been just like me? What kind of shoes would I be wearing?

I went inside. A rack on a far wall appeared as if it had a million pairs of black penny loafers resting on it. On a rack next to it was a sign that read, "CLEARANCE 50% OFF." Below the sign sat several "young" versions of Dad's shoes.

My mind was playing Ping-Pong. First Dad's old shoes and then the new ones. First the image of me keeping up with the "in" crowd at school. And then this image of Dad—tireless, selfless, almost Christlike in the sacrifices he was willing to make for his family. When it came to keeping up, which ideal was worth following?

I took a size ten from the clearance rack and darted to the checkout counter. Tax included, the shoes came to $6.13. I ran back to the shop and put Dad's new shoes on the seat in his car. I went and gave him the change I had left.

"I thought the shoes were nine ninety-five," he said.

"They were on sale." I took a broom from the nearby wall and started helping Dad sweep up. At five o'clock he signaled that it was time to go.

Dad picked up the box when we got in the car. When he opened it he just stared without saying a word. He looked first at the shoes and then at me.

"I thought you were going to get those penny loafers," he said.

"I was, Dad, but—" I couldn't explain the rest. How could I tell Dad that his was the image I had chosen to follow? Or when it came to keeping up, I wanted to try to keep up with the very best? I wanted to be more like the good man God had given me for a father.

Dad put his hand on my shoulder and we sat looking at each other for a moment. Nothing else was said. Dad started the car and we went home.

THE GIFT OF DAD

JEFF JAPINGA

Here are two stories…one written in 1986 and one written in 2010 by the same man. One is about his father and the other about being a father—and each is about a gift.

1986

I grew up in Holland, Michigan, a small city on the shore of Lake Michigan. Holland is the home of Hope College, a school of 2,500 students. Now that it's June most of them are off at summer jobs or maybe just at the beach. Some of the Hope staff are still on hand, though, and a lot of summers I'd help out some of them.

I remember especially one of those hot August dog days. With football practice just a week away, the time had come for Bunko to paint side- and yard lines. Bunko's real name is Norman, and he's the athletic equipment manager at Hope. That August day I was his able assistant.

Lining a football field sounds simple. You cut the grass very short where the yard lines are to go, fill up a special vacuum sprayer with white paint, and then lay down twenty-five straight lines. Easy, right? Well, not on Bunko's field. You see, every line had to be perfectly straight. Extra care is what he expected of me.

We stretched a four-hundred-foot string across the grass to provide a guideline for the paint machine. All through that blistering afternoon, backs beginning to ache, we made sure every line was straight and square. What seemed to make this enterprise absurd was that in one week this field would be unceremoniously torn up by 125 pairs of football cleats. Why bother being so careful?

But that day set me straight about straight lines: Bunko's concern was committing ourselves to doing our best, no matter what we were doing. Straight lines were just one way of Bunko's proving this lesson. I've since seen the same care and diligence in the way he treats the hundreds of people he comes in contact with each week, whether it's the college president or a student who needs his shoulder pads repaired. Bunko's "office" is always buzzing with laughter; people feel good there.

Ask Bunko about this, and he'll tell you he's just an ordinary guy doing his best. And perhaps that's what it is. But I can tell you that Bunko has made life extra-ordinary for a lot of people—especially me—with his very ordinary creed.

Now that I'm working in New York City, I still try to live up to Bunko's creed. My job is finding good books, and when my pile of thick manuscripts seems as overwhelming as a big unlined field on a hot August day, I picture Bunko with his lining string, and then I realize that the pile deserves my best effort.

I owe Bunko a lot, and since June isn't just the month of graduation and empty college campuses, I'll make this last line about Bunko as straight as I can. Happy Father's Day, Dad.

2010

Two years ago I was offered a new job. It promised to be challenging and fulfilling and, yes, even fun—a tremendous opportunity and a blessing in every way. Well, every way but one: It was 142 miles from home, each way; 142 miles from my wife's ministry, 142 miles from my daughter's high school. Moving wasn't a viable option.

For weeks I wrestled with one key question: not salary or prestige or career tracks, but about being a dad. Was I being selfish to take the job? Didn't being a father take priority? How can you be a good father when you're not even home?

Twice I had the phone in my hand, ready to turn down the job, but hung up. Then one day I happened to find myself in the same room as someone I knew who was a terrific father. I wound my way over to him and when he turned and said hello, I told him about my situation. "What should I do?" I asked him.

He looked me straight in the eye and said, "You—and your daughter—don't need my advice. You need each other. If you can give each other that, as often as you can, with as much commitment as you can muster, you'll be fine."

I took the job. It's meant being away from home two, three, sometimes even four nights a week. That's been really hard on all of us. But here's what I've learned about being a father from being away: That while kids think they need a lot of stuff, what they need most is *you*! And there are a million different ways to give a bit of yourself every day, whether you're home or not.

A Father, a Son, and an Answer

Bob Greene

Passing through the Atlanta airport one morning, I caught one of those trains that take travelers from the main terminal to their boarding gates. Free, sterile, and impersonal, the trains run back and forth all day long. Not many people consider them fun, but on this Saturday I heard laughter.

At the front of the first car—looking out the window at the track that lay ahead—were a man and his son. We had just stopped to let off passengers, and the doors were closing again. "Here we go! Hold on to me tight," the father said. The boy, about five years old, made sounds of sheer delight.

Most people on the train were dressed for business trips or vacations—and the father and son were dressed in clothes that were just about as inexpensive as you could buy.

"Look there!" the father said to his son. "See that pilot? I bet he's walking to his plane." The son craned his neck to look.

As I got off, I remembered something I'd wanted to buy in the terminal. I was early for my flight, so I decided to go back.

I did—and just as I was about to reboard the train for my gate, I saw that the man and his son had returned too. I realized then that they hadn't been heading for a flight, but had just been riding the shuttle.

"You want to go home now?" the father asked.

"I want to ride some more!"

"More?" the father said, mock-exasperated but clearly pleased. "You're not tired?"

"This is fun!" his son said.

"All right," the father replied, and when a door opened we all got on.

There are parents who can afford to send their children to Europe or Disneyland, and the children turn out rotten. There are parents who live in million-dollar houses and give their children cars and swimming pools, yet something goes wrong. Rich and poor, black and white, so much goes wrong so often.

"Where are all these people going, Daddy?" the son asked.

"All over the world," came the reply. The other people in the airport were leaving for distant destinations or arriving at the ends of their journeys. The father and son, though, were just riding the shuttle together, making it exciting, sharing each other's company.

So many troubles in this country—so many questions about what to do.

The answer is so simple: parents who care enough to spend time, and to pay attention, and to try their best. It doesn't cost a cent, yet it is the most valuable thing in the world.

The train picked up speed, and the father pointed out something, and the boy laughed again—and the answer is so simple.

*Y*ERR OUT!
CLARK COTHERN

My father gave me a great example of self-control when I was a boy watching a church-league softball game.

Dad was forty-three at the time and very active. Though he wasn't known for hitting grand slams, he was good at placing the ball and beating the throw. Singles and doubles were his specialty, and he did the best he could with what he had.

This particular dusty, hot Phoenix evening, Dad poked a good one right over the second baseman's head, and the center fielder flubbed the snag and let the ball bloop between his legs.

My dad saw this as he rounded first base, so he poured on the steam. He was five feet ten inches, 160 pounds, and very fast. He figured that if he sprinted for third and slid, he could beat the throw.

Everyone was cheering as he sent two of his teammates over home plate. The center fielder finally got his feet under him and his fingers around the ball as Dad headed toward third. The throw came as hard and fast as the outfielder could fire it, and Dad started a long slide on that sunbaked infield. Dust flew everywhere.

The ball slammed into the third baseman's glove but on the other side of Dad—the outfield side—away from a clear view by the ump who was still at home plate. Our team's dugout was on the third base side of the diamond, and every one of the players had a clear view of the play.

Dad's foot slammed into third base a solid second before the ball arrived and before the third baseman tagged his leg. But much to the amazement—and then dismay—and then anger—of the team, the umpire, who hesitated slightly before making his call, yelled, "Yerr out!"

Instantly, every member of Dad's team poured onto the field and started shouting at once—Dad's teammates were intent on only one purpose: They wanted to win, and, by golly, they knew they were *right*!

The two runners who had crossed home plate before Dad was called out had brought the score to within one. If Dad was out—and we all knew he wasn't—his team was robbed of a single run.

With only one inning left, this one bad call could cost them the game.

But just as the fracas threatened to boil over into a mini-riot, Dad silenced the crowd. As the dust settled around him, he held up a hand. "Guys, stop!" he yelled. And then more gently, "There's more at stake here than being right. There's something more important here than winning a game. If the ump says I'm out, I'm *out*."

And with that, he dusted himself off, limped to the bench to get his glove (his leg was bruised from the slide), and walked back into left field all by himself, ready to begin the last inning. One by one, the guys on his team gave up the argument, picked up their own gloves, and walked out to their positions on the field.

I've got to tell you, I was both bewildered and proud that night. My dad's character was showing, and it sparkled. He may have been dusty, but I saw a diamond standing out there under the lights, a diamond more valuable than all the points his team might have scored.

For a few minutes that evening I was a rich kid, basking in my father's decision to be a man, to hold his tongue instead of wagging it, to settle the dust instead of settling a score. I knew his character at that selfless moment was worth more than all the gold-toned plastic trophies you could buy.

Dad held court that night and the verdict came down hard. He was convicted of being a man…and the evidence that proved it was his powerful use of that awe-inspiring weapon.

Self-control.

$\mathcal{B}$ARCELONA OLYMPICS 1992
IVAN MAISEL

Barcelona, Spain—Jim Redmond did what any father would do. His child needed help. It was that simple. The Olympic Games have the kind of security that thousands of policemen and metal detectors can offer. But no venue is safe when a father sees his son's dream drifting away.

"One minute I was running," Derek Redmond of Great Britain said. "The next thing was a pop. I went down."

Derek, twenty-six, had waited for this four-hundred-meter semifinal for at least four years. In Seoul, he had an Achilles tendon problem. He waited until a minute-and-a-half before the race began before he would admit he couldn't run.

In November 1990, Derek underwent operations on both Achilles tendons. He has had five surgeries in all. But he came back. In the first two rounds he had run 45.02 and 45.03, his fastest times in five years.

"I really wanted to compete in my first Olympics," Redmond said. "I was feeling great. It just came out of the blue."

Halfway around the track, Redmond lay sprawled across lane five, his right hamstring gone bad.

Redmond struggled to his feet and began hobbling around the track. The winner of the heat, defending Olympic champion Steve Lewis, had finished and headed toward the tunnel. So had the other six runners. But the last runner in the heat hadn't finished. He continued to run.

Jim Redmond (Derek's dad), sitting high in the stands at Olympic Stadium, saw Derek collapse".

"You don't need accreditation in an emergency," Redmond said.

So Redmond, a forty-nine-year-old machine shop owner in Northampton, ran down the steps and onto the track.

"I was thinking," Jim Redmond said, "I had to get him there so he could say he finished the semifinal."

The crowd realized that Derek Redmond was running the race of his life. Around the stands, from around the world, the fans stood and honored him with cheers.

At the final turn, Jim Redmond caught up to his son and put his arm around him. Derek leaned on his dad's right shoulder and sobbed. But they kept going. An usher attempted to intercede and escort Jim Redmond off the track. If ever a futile mission had been undertaken....

They crossed the finish line, father and son, arm in arm.

THE OAK TREE

MAX LUCADO

On a recent trip to my hometown I took some time to go see a tree. "A live oak tree," my dad had called it (pronounced with the accent on "live"). It was nothing more than a sapling, so thin I could wrap my hand around it and touch my middle finger to my thumb. The West Texas wind scattered the fall leaves and caused me to zip up my coat. There is nothing colder than a prairie wind, especially in a cemetery.

"A special tree," I said to myself, "with a special job." I looked around. The cemetery was lined with elms but no oaks. The ground was dotted with tombstones but no trees. Just this one. A special tree for a special man.

About three years ago Daddy began noticing a steady weakening of his muscles. It began in his hands. He then felt it in his calves. Next his arms thinned a bit.

He mentioned his condition to my brother-in-law, who is a physician. My brother-in-law, alarmed, sent him to a specialist. The specialist conducted a lengthy battery of tests—blood, neurological, and muscular—and he reached his conclusion. Lou Gehrig's disease. A devastating crippler. No one knows the cause or the cure. The only sure thing about it is its cruelty and accuracy.

I looked down at the plot of ground that would someday entomb my father. Daddy always wanted to be buried under an oak tree so he brought this one. "Special order from the valley," he had boasted. "Had to get special permission from the city council to put it here." (That wasn't hard in this dusty oil-field town where everybody knows everybody.)

The lump got tighter in my throat. A lesser man might have been angry. Another man might have given up. But Daddy didn't. He knew that his days were numbered, so he began to get his house in order.

The tree was only one of the preparations he made. He improved the house for Mom by installing a sprinkler system and a garage door opener and by painting the trim. He got the will updated. He verified the insurance and retirement policies. He bought some stock to go toward his grandchildren's education. He planned his funeral. He bought cemetery plots for himself and Mom. He prepared his kids through words of assurance and letters of love. And last of all, he bought the tree. A live oak tree. (Pronounced with the accent on "live.")

Final acts. Final hours. Final words.

They reflect a life well lived.

The final hours are passing now. The gentle flame on his candle grows weaker and weaker. He lies in peace. His body dying, his spirit living. No longer can he get out of bed. He has chosen to live his last days at home. It won't be long. Death's windy draft will soon exhaust the flickering candle, and it will be over.

I looked one last time at the slender oak. I touched it as if it had been hearing my thoughts. "Grow," I whispered. "Grow strong. Stand tall. Yours is a valued treasure."

As I drove home through the ragged oil-field patchwork, I kept thinking about that tree. Though feeble, the decades will find it strong. Though slender, the years will add thickness and strength. Its last years will be its best. Just like my father's. Just like my Master's. "It is so much easier to die like Jesus if you have lived like Him for a lifetime."

"Grow, young tree." My eyes were misting. "Stand strong. Yours is a valued treasure."

He was awake when I got home. I leaned over his bed. "I checked on the tree," I told him. "It's growing."

He smiled.

$\mathcal{M}$Y DAD

$\mathcal{C}$HARLES SWINDOLL

My dad died last night.

He left like he had lived. Quietly. Graciously. With dignity. Without demands or harsh words or even a frown, he surrendered himself—a tired, frail, humble gentleman—into the waiting arms of his Savior. Death, selfish and cursed, enemy of man, won another battle.

As I stroked the hair from his forehead and kissed him good-bye, a hundred boyhood memories played around in my head.

- When I learned to ride a bike, he was there.
- When I wrestled with the multiplication tables, his quick wit erased the hassle.
- When I discovered the adventure of driving a car, he was near, encouraging me.
- When I got my first job (delivering newspapers), he informed me how to increase my subscriptions and win the prize. It worked!
- When I did a hitch in the Marine Corps, the discipline I had learned from him made the transition easier.

From him I learned to seine for shrimp. How to gig flounder and catch trout and red fish. How to open oyster shells and fix crab gumbo…and chili…and popcorn…and make rafts out of old inner tubes and gunny sacks. I was continually amazed at his ability to do things like tie fragile mantles on the old Coleman lantern, keep a fire going in the rain, play the harmonica with his hands behind his back and keep three strong-willed kids from tearing down the house.

Last night I realized I had him to thank for my deep love for America. And for knowing how to tenderly care for my wife. And for laughing at impossibilities. And for some of the habits I have picked up, like approaching people with a positive spirit rather than a negative one, staying with a task until it is finished, taking good care of my personal belongings, keeping my shoes shined, speaking up rather than mumbling, respecting authority, and standing alone (if necessary) in support of my personal convictions rather than giving in to more popular opinions. For these things I am deeply indebted to the man who raised me.

Certain smells and sounds now instantly remind me of my dad. Oyster stew. The ocean breeze. Smoke from an expensive cigar. The nostalgic whine of a harmonica. A camping lantern and white gas. Car polish. Fun songs from the thirties and forties. Freshly mowed grass. A shrill whistle from a father to his kids around supper time. And Old Spice aftershave.

Because a father affects his family so permanently, I think I understand better than ever what the Scripture means when Paul wrote:

> Having thus a fond affection for you, we were well-pleased to impart to you not only the gospel of God but also our own lives, because you had become very dear to us...just as you know how we were exhorting and encouraging and imploring each one of you as a father would his own children, so that you may walk in a manner worthy of the God who calls you into His own kingdom and glory (1 Thessalonians 2:8, 11-12).

Admittedly, much of my dad's instruction was indirect—by model rather than by explicit statement. I do not recall his overt declaration of love as clearly as I do his demonstrations of it. His life revolved around my mother, the darling and delight of his life. Of that I am sure. When she left over nine years ago, something of him died as well. And so—to her he has been joined and they are together, with our Lord, in the closest possible companionship one can imagine.

In this my sister, my brother, and I find our greatest comfort—they are now forever *with the Lord*—eternally freed from pain and aging and death. Secure in Jesus Christ our

Lord. Absent from the body and at home with Him. And with each other.

Last night I said good-bye. I'm still trying to believe it. You'd think it would be easy, since his illness has persisted for more than three years. How well I remember the Sunday he suffered that first in a series of strokes as I was preaching. God granted him several more years to teach many of us to appreciate the things we tend to take for granted.

He leaves in his legacy a well-marked Bible I treasure, a series of feelings that I need to deepen my roots, and a thousand memories that comfort me as I replace denial with acceptance and praise.

I await heaven's gate opening in the not-too-distant future. So do other Christians, who anxiously await Christ's return. Most of them anticipate hearing the soft strum of a harp or the sharp, staccato blast of a trumpet.

Not me. I will hear the nostalgic whine of a harmonica... held in the hands of the man who died last night...*or did he*? The memories are as fresh as this morning's sunrise.

ONE MORE DANCE
CHRISTOPHER SCHONHARDT

I was a senior in high school when my dad passed away in 1975. Mom had sorted through his clothes and asked me to bring the boxes downstairs for pickup by the local disabled veterans group. *I should save something,* I thought. But Dad was much bigger than I was.

I stared down at one box and saw his brown wing tips, the left heel worn down more than the right, a reminder of Dad's boyhood polio. Dad was a mechanic who wore practical shoes; this one old pair of dress shoes only came out of the closet for church and special occasions. The tops of the shoes were scuffed and as I ran my fingers across the leather, I found myself thinking back to how those scuffs came to be.

We had attended a wedding with my parents' friends Lorraine and Matthew. Multiple sclerosis confined Lorraine to a wheelchair; the disease had also sapped her spirit. As her husband wheeled her into the reception, the eager greetings of the other guests dropped to whispers. "It's a shame," I heard someone say. "She was a dancer—and quite a good one."

The band had been playing for a while when my father bent down to Lorraine's ear. "May I have this dance?" he asked. In one smooth motion Dad lifted her from the wheelchair and Matthew placed her shoes on top of Dad's wing tips. Everyone watched the couple glide across the dance floor. Lorraine, supported by my father's strong arms, stood smiling, eyes closed, head tilted back.

After the last song faded, Dad and Lorraine whirled toward her wheelchair and he gently lowered her into it. Beaming, Lorraine gave my father a vigorous hug.

Now, as I carried my father's wing tips downstairs with the rest of his things, I thought of what he had left me, what I would save. It would be the memories of a man who always tried to make a difference in others' lives.

THE HEART OF THE MATTER

HE DREAMS, HE PLANS.
HE STRUGGLES THAT
WE MIGHT HAVE THE BEST.
HIS SACRIFICE IS QUIET,
HIS LIFE IS LOVE EXPRESSED.

~AUTHOR UNKNOWN

A POINTER NAMED CHEYENNE
CATHERINE MOORE

"Watch out! You nearly broadsided that car!" my father yelled at me. "Can't you do anything right?"

Those words hurt worse than blows. I turned my head toward the elderly man in the seat beside me, daring me to challenge him. A lump rose in my throat as I averted my eyes. I wasn't prepared for another battle.

"I saw the car, Dad. Please don't yell at me when I'm driving." My voice was measured and steady, sounding far calmer than I really felt. Dad glared at me, then turned away and settled back.

At home I left Dad in front of the television and went outside to collect my thoughts. Dark, heavy clouds hung in the air with a promise of rain. The rumble of distant thunder seemed to echo my inner turmoil. What could I do about him?

Dad had been a lumberjack in Washington and Oregon. He had enjoyed being outdoors and had reveled in pitting his strength against the forces of nature. He had entered grueling lumberjack competitions, and he had placed often. The shelves in his house were filled with trophies that attested to his prowess.

The years marched on relentlessly. The first time he couldn't lift a heavy log he joked about it; but later that same day I saw him outside alone, straining to lift it. He became irritable whenever anyone teased him about his advancing age, or when he couldn't do something he had done as a younger man.

Four days after his sixty-seventh birthday he had a heart attack. An ambulance sped him to the hospital while a paramedic administered CPR to keep blood and oxygen flowing. At the hospital Dad was rushed into an operating room. He was lucky; he survived.

But something inside Dad died. His zest for life was gone. He obstinately refused to follow doctor's orders. Suggestions and offers of help were turned aside with sarcasm and insults. The number of visitors thinned, then finally stopped altogether. Dad was left alone.

My husband Dick and I asked Dad to come live with us on our small farm. We hoped the fresh air and rustic atmosphere would help him adjust. Within a week after he moved in, I regretted the invitation. It seemed nothing was satisfactory. He criticized everything I did. I became frustrated and moody. Soon I was taking out my pent-up anger on Dick. We began to bicker and argue. Alarmed, Dick sought out our pastor and explained the situation. The clergyman set up weekly counseling appointments for us. At the close of each session he prayed, asking God to soothe Dad's troubled mind. But the months wore on and God was silent.

A raindrop struck my cheek. I looked up into the gray sky. Somewhere up there was "God." Although I believed a Supreme Being had created the universe, I had difficulty believing that God cared about the tiny human beings on this earth. I was tired of waiting for a God who didn't answer. Something had to be done and it was up to me to do it.

The next day I sat down with the phone book and methodically called each of the mental-health clinics listed in the yellow pages. I explained my problem to the sympathetic voices that answered. In vain. Just when I was giving up hope, one of the voices suddenly exclaimed, "I just read something that might help you! Let me go get the article." I listened as she read. The article described a remarkable study done at a nursing home. All of the patients were under treatment for chronic depression. Yet their attitudes had improved dramatically when they were given responsibility for a dog.

I drove to the animal shelter that afternoon. After I filled out a questionnaire, a uniformed officer led me to the kennels. The odor of disinfectant stung my nostrils as I moved down the row of pens. Each contained five to seven dogs. Longhaired dogs, curly-haired dogs, black dogs, spotted dogs—all jumped up, trying to reach me. I studied each one but rejected one after the other for various reasons—too big, too small, too much hair. As I neared the last pen a dog in the shadows of the far corner struggled to his feet, walked to the front of the run and sat down. It was a pointer, one of the dog world's aristocrats. But this was a caricature of the breed. Years had etched his face and muzzle with shades of gray. His hipbones jutted out in lopsided triangles. It was his eyes that caught and held my attention. Calm and clear, they beheld me unwaveringly.

I pointed to the dog. "Can you tell me about him?" The officer looked, then shook his head in puzzlement.

"He's a funny one. Appeared out of nowhere and sat in front of the gate. We brought him in, figuring someone would be right down to claim him. That was two weeks ago and we've heard nothing. His time is up tomorrow." He gestured helplessly.

As the words sank in I turned to the man in horror. "You mean you're going to kill him?"

"Ma'am," he said gently, "that's our policy. We don't have room for every unclaimed dog."

I looked at the pointer again. The calm brown eyes awaited my decision. "I'll take him," I said.

I drove home with the dog on the front seat beside me. When I reached the house I honked the horn twice. I was helping my prize out of the car when Dad shuffled onto the front porch.

"Ta-da! Look what I got for you, Dad!" I said excitedly.

Dad looked, then wrinkled his face in disgust. "If I had wanted a dog I would have gotten one. And I would have picked out a better specimen than that bag of bones. Keep it! I don't want it!" Dad waved his arm scornfully and turned back toward the house.

Anger rose inside me. It squeezed together my throat muscles and pounded into my temples. I followed Dad, dragging the dog with me.

"You had better get used to him, Dad. He's staying!" Dad ignored me. "Did you hear me, old man?" I screamed. At those words Dad whirled angrily, his hands clenched at his sides, his eyes narrowed and blazing with hate. We stood glaring at each other like duelists when suddenly the pointer pulled free from my grasp. He wobbled toward my dad and sat down in front of him. Then slowly, carefully, he raised his paw.

Dad's lower jaw trembled as he stared at the uplifted paw. Confusion replaced the anger in his eyes. The pointer waited patiently. Then Dad was on his knees hugging the animal.

It was the beginning of a warm and intimate friendship. Dad named the pointer Cheyenne. Together he and Cheyenne explored the community. They spent long hours walking down dusty lanes. They spent reflective moments on the banks of streams, angling for tasty trout. They even started to attend

Sunday services together, Dad sitting in a pew and Cheyenne lying quietly at his feet.

Dad and Cheyenne were inseparable throughout the next three years. Dad's bitterness faded and he and Cheyenne made many friends. Then late one night I was startled to feel Cheyenne's cold nose burrowing through our bed covers. He had never before come into our bedroom at night. I woke Dick, put on my robe and ran into my father's room. Dad lay in his bed, his face serene. But his spirit had left quietly sometime during the night.

Two days later my shock and grief deepened when I discovered Cheyenne lying dead beside Dad's bed. I wrapped his still form in the rag rug he had slept on. As Dick and I buried him near a favorite fishing hole, I silently thanked the dog for the help he had given me in restoring Dad's peace of mind.

The morning of Dad's funeral dawned overcast and dreary. *This day looks like the way I feel*, I thought, as I walked down the aisle to the pews reserved for family. I was surprised to see the many friends Dad and Cheyenne had made filling the church. The pastor began his eulogy. It was a tribute to both Dad and the dog who had changed his life. And then the pastor turned to Hebrews 13:2. "'Be not forgetful to entertain strangers: for thereby some have entertained angels unawares.' I've often thanked God for sending that angel," he said.

For me, the past dropped into place, completing a puzzle that I had not seen before...the sympathetic voice that had just read the right article...Cheyenne's unexpected appearance at the animal shelter...his calm acceptance and complete devotion to my father...and the proximity of their deaths....

And suddenly I understood, I knew, that God had answered my prayers after all.

THE OLD KING

BRIAN DOYLE

My vast Irish-American clan was at the dinner table on a bright summer evening, grandparents at either end and a gaggle of sons and daughters-in-law and mobs of children in between and a baby on a lap somewhere. Hilarity and hubbub were in the air.

"Pass the ketchup."

"This is terrific pasta. Who made this pasta?"

"Who's on the dishwashing crew?"

"What time is the game tonight?"

A story started as my sister got up to get more food and my brothers were laughing and correcting one another in loud voices getting louder. My dad, down at the end of the table where the king sits, cleared his throat and started to add to the story, but no one heard him. The conversation swirled on without him, and he subsided without being able to say his piece. I noticed this when it happened, but I said nothing.

Dad leaned back in his chair and didn't say anything for a while. I realized later that something important in the family had come to pass at that moment, and that I wasn't brave enough to force the table to listen to the old king, and that I loved that man immensely for the king he had been—calm, generous, trustworthy, graceful.

If I am someday even a scant shadow of the great man my father is, I will thank God ten times a day for ten thousand years.

LOOK, DADDY, I CAN FLY!

BECKY FREEMAN

Although I love the slinky, silky gowns my husband gives me every holiday season, this year I asked if he might give me something a little less breezy. I was particularly interested in sleepwear that would wrap warm and snugly around my cold, cold feet.

Thinking it would be a cute joke, Scott gave me a pair of "woman size" pink and white "feety" pajamas—in a teddy-bear print. Christmas evening, I stole away to the bedroom and tried them on just for fun. As I put one foot and then another into the pajama legs, I drifted back to the very first memory I have as a child. I could almost hear my daddy—as he sounded nearly thirty-five years ago—softly singing, "Put your little foot, put your little foot, put your little foot right here…" as I stood on my bed while he helped me into my footed pj's.

My father is one man who has managed, all his life, to keep his child-heart pumping strong.

One rainy spring afternoon, when I was about eleven, I went out to the garage to find my father ascending a ladder into the attic. Though Daddy was sentimental, he was *not* a handyman, so the sight of the ladder provoked my curiosity. Then he crooked his finger in a silent gesture that I knew meant, "Come along, but be quiet."

I followed him up into the attic and sat down beside him, curious as to the nature of our exploration. But all my dad said was, "*Shh*...listen." Then I heard it. The rain, pattering overhead—amplified by our nearness to the rooftop.

"I come up here whenever it rains," Daddy said softly. It was cool and comforting, a tender moment caught—like a snapshot—in my mind.

To my pleasant surprise, my husband turned out to be a rain-on-the-roof kind of guy too. He even built our bed so that the head of it fits snug against a large picture window. At night, if the full moon is shining or a soft rain is falling, Scott pulls up the blinds and raises the window and whispers, "*Shh*... Becky. Listen." And this, I believe, is part of the reason why the two men I love most in the whole world are my daddy and my husband.

Another amazing thing about Daddy: In all my years, I cannot ever recall my father criticizing me. Not once. Always, he would praise and encourage my efforts—however crazy, however childish.

Not long ago I had a dream; it was a recurring dream I've had for years. In it I can fly. I love these dreams, and while I'm in them, I cannot understand why other people don't just float themselves up to the sky and join me. It is so easy, nothing to it at all. Most of the time I just spread out my arms and take off, but in one of my dreams I piloted a Frisbee. Now *that* was fun!

But the last dream I had was especially realistic. Once again I was flying, and in my dream I thought to myself, *This is ridiculous. Nobody else is flying except me. I need to find out if this is real or if this is just my imagination.*

So I flew to my parents' home, knocked on the door, and floated up to the ceiling. Then I hovered over my father, who was looking up at me, not at all surprised to find me up there, and I said, "Daddy, listen. You've got to tell me the truth. I really think I'm flying. It feels so real. But I'm worried that this might just be all a dream."

My daddy's answer was swift and sure. "Honey," he said, "it's no dream. You're flying, all right."

When I woke up I laughed, but then tears welled in my eyes. *How marvelous*, I thought, *that even in my subconscious, in spite of all logic to the contrary, I have a father who believes I can fly.*

For Father's Day last year, I could not find a card that seemed to fit how I felt about Daddy. However, I came across a scene in a children's book that turned out to be perfect. It was a scene with Piglet and Winnie-the-Pooh, walking side by side toward a setting sun. Their short conversation summed up exactly how I felt about my father through the years.

Piglet sidled up to Pooh from behind.

"Pooh," he whispered.

"Yes, Piglet?"

"Nothing," said Piglet, taking Pooh's paw. "I just wanted to be sure of you."

My dad has been like Pooh to me, his Little Girl-Piglet. Oh, we don't chitchat a whole lot, not like my mother and I do, anyway. But in every memory involving my father—from the time he sang, "Put your little foot" as he helped me into my footed pj's, until this latest dream where he assured me that, yes, I could really fly—my father has been there in the shadows, cheering me on. He has given me the steadfast confidence that always, and forever, I can be sure of him.

My Gift from Dad

Steve Dwinnells

I have a special box. It's a little, wooden box with two small, shiny handles and a tiny padlock. It's simple—no fancy engravings, no high-gloss finish, no felt-covered bottom. The edges don't fit together very well, the hinges on the lid have begun to squeak.

But it's my box, and every now and again I take the small key and unlock the padlock. As I raise the lid, the box releases its special memories, and the memories take me back to another time and another place.

Inside the box are a few knickknacks and a letter. Not much value in the world's eyes, maybe, but a priceless treasure to me. This box was a gift from my dad.

One Christmas Dad made boxes for all three of us boys. He wasn't much of a carpenter. Some of the pieces aren't cut exactly right, and the joints don't quite fit together.

But to me, a master carpenter couldn't have made anything better. The box's perfection isn't in its form, but in the motivation behind the making of it.

The box was made by big, callused hands that knew hard work; by a mind that understood what responsibility means;

by a warm heart that loved me. Inside the box is a handwritten letter addressed to me by my dad. The letter will never be published or nominated for a literary award. It is just a simple letter expressing a tenderness that Dad didn't know how to say very well aloud. It is a note telling me how proud he was of me and that he loved me. In the only way that he knew, he told me that he was glad I was his son.

Dad died a few days after Christmas that year. He didn't leave much money or a big home. But he did leave me that box. With a simple box and a simple message, he left me his love.

As the years have come and gone, the box has taken on even greater value to me as I have come to realize what it really symbolizes. It is a reminder that only the gifts of our hearts hold enduring worth.

The smoothly sanded, varnished sides represent the hard work and the perseverance that I ought to strive for. The strength of the wood epitomizes the lasting strength that I need as I struggle through life's difficulties. The blemishes and the flaws reveal to me that perfection lies not in outward appearances. And like the letter inside, the box shows that warmth and love come from within, from the heart.

Like the box, I have nicks and rough edges, and my joints don't match up well. But just as a letter of fatherly love fills that box, I know that the perfect love of God fills me, making me a masterpiece.

BENCHED
JAMES ROBISON

I remember an occasion when our son Randy played extremely well in Little League baseball. He had actually batted .500 that year and, as I recall, had only two singles. He was primarily hitting doubles—and also some triples and home runs. He was consistently driving the ball up against the outfield fence on one or two bounces—good enough for extra bases in Little League. He was having the year of his life, and this daddy felt pretty puffed up about it all....

Yet even with the great year he was having, Randy seemed to be on the bench quite a bit as the coaches tried to play as many boys as possible. Always polite, Randy had a great attitude about it, and seemed content to give others their turn in the spotlight. He wasn't struggling a bit.

But I was!

More than once, I told the coach how I felt about it. How could he pull a kid who was having such a great year? How could he replace him with boys who didn't care nearly as much or play nearly as well? Didn't he want to win? Wasn't he sending the wrong signals by benching the kids who were playing the hardest and best?

As a matter of fact, there really were some wrong signals on that field. But they weren't coming from the coach. It was my own impatient, win-at-all-costs attitude that was sending the wrong signals.

Randy didn't like having his dad in the coach's face. It made him nervous and embarrassed him. He would find himself looking over his shoulder, wondering how Dad was going to react to this or that decision. It was something of a shadow right in the midst of that superb year. Down in my heart, I knew that my attitude bothered him—and I asked the Lord to help me back off a little.

When Randy made the all-star team we were all as excited as could be. I can remember flying home and getting to one of the all-star games just a little bit late. As I walked up to the ball diamond from the parking lot, I could see that Randy's team was already in the field and my heart started pounding a little bit harder.

But where was Randy? I approached the bleachers and there he was, sitting by himself on the bench. Good night! It didn't make sense. This was the kid who led the league in batting averages and had played so well in the field. And he was starting the all-star game *on the bench*?

Randy looked unsmilingly over his shoulder as he watched me take my seat in the bleachers. Seeing the expression on his face, I honestly felt as though I could read his mind. He was thinking: *Oh man, I know Dad is really disappointed and upset to see me on the bench. Dear God, please don't let him say anything or let it show.*

By the grace of God, that was one of those moments when I finally got it right. While I was still in my car driving from the airport to the game, I felt strongly impressed that I somehow needed to convey to that young man how thoroughly proud I was of him—and that he didn't need to "perform" to get my approval.

I walked over to the fence and leaned over. My boy looked up. Somewhat apprehensively.

"Randy," I said, "I want you to know I am just as proud of you sitting right here on this bench as I would be if you were starting third base and hitting home runs. There's no way I could ever be more proud of you. You're my son, and you don't have to do anything to please me or to gain my approval. You've got it a hundred percent. I love you, Son."

Tears filled his eyes and he smiled. Somehow I knew I had touched a chord. And with thanks in my heart to God, I knew I had done exactly the right thing.

BETWEEN THE LINES

CHARLOTTE ADELSPERGER

After a moving memorial service for my beloved father, Walter Rist, our family gathered at our childhood home to be with Mother. Memories of Dad whirled in my mind. I could see his warm brown eyes and contagious smile. I envisioned all six-feet-four of him in hat and coat, headed to teach his classes at the college. Quickly, a new scene flashed in my mind of Dad in a T-shirt playing ball with Alberta, Wally, and me on the front lawn. He was swinging a baseball bat, hitting long flies to us kids—year ago.

But special memories couldn't push away the dark shadows of separation from the one we loved.

Later in the evening, while looking for something in a closet, we found a paper sack marked, "Charlotte's Scrapbook." In curiosity, I opened it. There it was—my "Inspiration from Here and There" scrapbook I had kept as a teenager. I had forgotten all about it until that moment when I leafed through the pages of pasted pictures from magazines and church bulletins. They were punctuated with clippings of famous quotes, Bible verses, and poetry. *This was me as a teenager,* I thought. *My heart's desires.*

Then I saw something I'd never seen before—my father's handwriting penciled on page after page! My throat tightened as I read the little notes Dad had slipped in to communicate with me. They were love messages and words of wisdom. I had no idea when he had written these, but *this* was the day to find them!

On the first page, Dad wrote, "Life is never a burden if love prevails." My chin quivered. I trembled. I could hardly believe the timeliness of his words. I flipped the pages for more.

Under a picture of a bride being given away by her father, my dad wrote, "How proud I was to walk down the aisle with you, Charlotte!"

Near a copy of the Lord's Prayer he had scrawled, "I have always found the strength I needed, but only with God's help. He has never failed me." What a comfort!

I turned to a picture of a young boy sitting on the grass with a gentle collie resting its head on his lap. Beneath it were these words, "I had a collie like this one when I was a boy. She was run over by a streetcar and disappeared. Three weeks later she came home, limping with a broken leg, her tail cut off. Her name was Queenie. She lived for many more years. I watched her give birth to seven puppies. I loved her very much.—Dad."

My moist eyes blurred as I read another page. "Dear Charlotte, listen to your children! Let them talk. Hold Bob's hand whenever you can. Hold your children's hands. Much love will be transferred, much warmth to remember." What a treasure of guidance for me as a wife and mother! I clung to the words from my dad whose gentle big hand often held mine.

In those moments of paging through the scrapbook, incredible comfort was etched on the gray canvas of my life. On this, the day my father was buried, he had a loving "last word." Such a precious surprise, somehow allowed by God, cast victorious light on the shadows of my grief. I was able to walk on, covered by fresh beacons of strength.

$\mathcal{I}$'m Daddy's Girl

Becky Freeman

One evening not long ago, my husband stayed home with the children while I went to the grocery store. Shopping for a family of six when four of them are males takes a while, so it was late when I got home. When I walked into the house, all was dark and unusually quiet. After setting down a bag of groceries, I tiptoed into the bedroom, lighted by the soft glow of the moon sifting through the window. Scott was lying there, hands folded behind his head, staring at the ceiling. He seemed so pensive I immediately thought something was bothering him.

"Hey," I said softly and sat down on the bed beside him. "What's the matter?"

"Aw, I was just thinking about my daughter," he grinned sheepishly. "And how much I love her."

Evidently it had been a very good evening. "What happened with Rachel tonight?" I asked.

"Well," he sighed and searched for words to convey what he was feeling. "I had built a fire outside to burn some excess wood, and the telephone rang. It turned out to be a tough discussion with someone and I was upset. So I went outside to unwind by the fire, and, before long, our little girl came out of the house and snuggled by my side.

"Dad," she told me, "you look like you could use a hug." He paused briefly and breathed a contented sigh.

"She's my little sweetheart, you know."

"I know," I smiled as I rubbed the back of my husband's neck. "And I hope she always will be."

The next evening Scott came home from work and found me asleep on the couch. He woke me by tickling my nose with a long-stemmed red rose. Before I could properly gush over it, Rachel strolled in from her room, beaming from ear to ear. Her strawberry-blonde curls *boing-yoinging* happily as she plopped down on the sofa beside me. In her small, slender hands she held a lavender basket of fresh daisies and pink carnations. Tucked into the arrangement was a card in Scott's handwriting.

"Thanks for the hug," it read.

Rachel's brown eyes twinkled, and she smiled triumphantly in my direction. "You just got *one* flower. Daddy gave *me* a whole basket!"

Defining Dad

Any man can be a father, but it takes a special person to be a dad.

~Author Unknown

THANKS TO THE FATHERS

OSCAR GREENE

My interview for a security clearance was going well. The interviewer and I liked each other. Then she asked, "Tell me about your father."

Without thinking, I answered, "I never knew my father." The interviewer blushed and passed quickly to the next question.

Perhaps it was my hunger for warmth, attention, and companionship that triggered my blunt response. Mother and Father divorced before I was two. Mother remarried when I was seven. My stepfather was an excellent provider who felt that giving encouragement and praise was silly and unnecessary. From time to time I wondered about my "real" father, but this was curiosity rather than yearning. Over the years I made no attempt to find him. Now I wrote to my mother to let her know about my angry feelings.

I received my security clearance; I also received a letter from Mother. "I can understand your anger, Son," she wrote. "Try not to be too critical. Try to remember all the fine people who reached out to help you."

My thoughts raced back to the Reverend Gardiner M. Day, our minister, who gave me a job during the Great Depression; to Edward Welch, my high-school English teacher, who nurtured my talent for public speaking while teaching me the joys of reading and writing; to John B. Clark, my high-school principal, who helped me get into college with a much-needed scholarship; to Herbert Kenny, arts editor at The Boston Globe, who hired me to be a book reviewer; to Dave McKinney, the aerospace engineer who selected me to serve in the Project Gemini space program.

Suddenly, I was aware that I had many fathers, caring men who guided and encouraged me, each in his own way. So on this Father's Day, I give thanks to my Father in heaven, to the father I never knew, to my stepfather and to all the fatherly men who have touched my life.

CELEBRATING FATHER'S DAY
MARION BOND WEST

Growing up in Elberton, Georgia, my childhood was happy,
except for one particular holiday. I dreaded it, pretended it
didn't exist, tried to ignore it. But no matter what I did, a secret
longing remained in my heart: You can't celebrate Father's Day.
Your father's dead. You don't even have a real memory of him.

As an adult I still couldn't come to terms with that longing.
I still wanted to celebrate Father's Day with my own daddy.

Then, a few years ago, the Atlanta Journal-Constitution
invited readers to submit memories of their father's shoes and
what the shoes had meant to them as children. My memory was
as real as if it had happened yesterday. I was about eight and
accidentally discovered a pair of my father's shoes hidden way
back in my mother's closet. My paper dolls suddenly forgotten,
I touched the dusty shoes tenderly, examined them thoroughly
in the sunlight, laced and unlaced them, and finally cradled
one in each arm.

I mailed my memory to the newspaper because it satisfied
something in me that I didn't fully understand. Lo and behold,
the newspaper sent a photographer to my house. He took

pictures of me holding an eight-by-ten photograph of the father I'd never known.

That Father's Day, I crept out before sunrise and found our newspaper in the driveway. There, in living color, was a picture of me with my father. And, for the first time, I genuinely celebrated Father's Day.

LEARNING TO LOVE

BERNARD "RICHIE" THOMASSEN
AS TOLD TO HEATHER BLACK

Trissa came up to me a few minutes before math class. "Hey Richie, you know about cars," she said. "Mine's making a funny noise. Could you take a look at it?"

"Sure," I said, and then another girl named Arielle spoke up.

"Can I come watch?" she asked. "I want to learn how to fix cars too."

A year ago I didn't even know what a distributor cap was. But nowadays my friends come to me with their car problems. They think I'm some kind of expert, but my new dad Roger— he's the real expert. Roger also taught me more important stuff—about life and love, and what it truly means to become a man.

My real dad left when I was only a baby, and for fifteen years it was just my mom and me. When the other guys played football with their dads, I could only watch. And it was a little embarrassing going on fishing trips when my mom was the only woman there. But I convinced myself it didn't really matter. After all, how could I miss having a dad when I'd never had a dad to lose?

I was happy when we moved from Brooklyn to Nyack, New York, where my mom worked for Sears. There was a lot more room to ride bikes and play ball, and at school there were coaches who taught me how to swing a bat and catch a pass—you know, the sort of things your dad's supposed to teach you.

I made a lot of new friends in Nyack, and my mom even started dating. Some of the guys were okay; others I thought were total jerks. But the night Mom and I met Roger at a New Year's Eve party, I didn't know what to think.

Roger was six feet three inches tall and 250 pounds, with long hair and a beard. He was loud and a little hard of hearing, and his forearms were as big around as my thighs.

"Nice to meet you," Roger boomed when somebody introduced us. When he shook my hand, it disappeared inside his huge paw, callused and scarred from years of construction work and working in the boiler room of a Navy ship during the Vietnam War.

I thought Roger was one scary dude, but on the drive home when we talked about him, Mom got sort of dreamy. "He's actually very gentle," she said, and told me how sensitive Roger had seemed when he talked about his two sons who had drowned seventeen years before in a canoeing accident.

I still thought Roger was a little freaky, but a few nights later when he called I tried not to make a face as I handed Mom the phone. They talked for hours, and a few nights after that Roger took Mom to dinner. I didn't know whether to feel happy for her or worried that she'd maybe flipped her lid.

Then one night Roger was sitting in our living room waiting for Mom to get ready while I was talking to my grandparents on the phone. I told my grandma I loved her when I finished talking to her, but to my grandfather I just said good-bye.

Hanging up, I was surprised when Roger cleared his throat to speak—and even more surprised by what he said. "I know why you didn't tell your grandfather you love him," he began. "It's because he's a guy, and you were embarrassed to tell him how you feel."

Roger talked some about his sons who had drowned. "Not a day passes when I don't wish I'd said 'I love you' to them even more than I did. 'I love you' isn't just something you say to women," he said. Now I was really confused because here was this giant tough guy with tears rolling down his cheeks.

I still remember the first time Mom and I visited Roger's house. The place overflowed with old newspapers and magazines, and everywhere you turned there were broken toasters and televisions Roger had always meant to fix. Then we went out to the garage—and wow!

Ever since I was little I've loved taking things apart to see how they work. Radios, my Ghostbusters game—I could take them apart fine, but there were always parts left over when I tried to put them back together. And the only tools I ever had were the screwdrivers and pliers from the kitchen drawer.

But Roger's garage was one big workshop full of tools I'd never even seen before.

For the next hour, Roger showed me reciprocating saws, ratchets, and about a thousand other tools. "Maybe one day we can work on a project together," he said, and I forced myself not to smile because what if he never did? What if Roger was just pretending to like me to impress my mom?

I guess you could say Roger swept my mom off her feet because it wasn't long before we were packing our things to move into his house. Roger and I spent days hauling junk to the dump in his pickup. We also refinished the floors.

A few weeks later, Roger taught me how to work a stick shift driving back and forth in the driveway. Then we went to the Department of Motor Vehicles to get my learner's permit.

Another day Roger brought home an old Ford Escort that barely ran. "We'll fix her up together, and then you'll have something to drive," he said. This time I didn't even try to hide my smile.

When we discovered the Escort's transmission was shot, Roger bought a used transmission from the junkyard, and we jacked up the car and swapped it out with the old one. It was hard work, especially for a tall, skinny kid like me. But one night Mom gripped my forearm and smiled. "You're putting on muscle," she said.

"I know," I said proudly, and I owed it all to Roger.

Even after we got it running, Roger and I spent hours tinkering with my car, and we did a lot of talking while we worked. Roger told me about when he was my age and he and his dog Silus used to sit beside the tracks for hours watching the trains roll by, and how he'd worked at a gas station for free just so he could learn to fix cars.

Roger also talked about some of the many kids he'd taken into his home over the years—abused kids, kids strung out on drugs, even a few who had spent time in jail. Roger helped these guys through some pretty tough times, and many of them have grown up to become successful businessmen, policemen, and firemen. They still come by with their wives and families to thank him.

These days our house is full of tiny parts from a piano Roger and I are rebuilding because we both want to know what makes it work. We also love going for long drives through the country, stopping at farms to check out the animals while we talk about life. Sometimes we talk about girls and stuff like that, but after hearing stories about the kids Roger helped, he didn't have to warn me about abusing drugs and alcohol. I don't want to screw up my life or wind up in prison. I want to grow up to be hard-working, honest, and caring—just like Roger.

Besides my mom, Roger is the only person I know who will always be there for me, no matter what. Thanks to Roger I've grown tougher on the outside, but inside I know it's okay to care about people and tell them so.

Last Father's Day, I wrote Roger a letter telling him how much he'd changed my life. "I never had a dad until I was a teenager, but now I have the greatest dad in the world," I wrote. "You've taken me places I never would have gone, both out in the world and inside myself, and your 'I love you's' are the most reassuring and wonderful words I've ever heard in my life."

Tomatoes from Dad
Joyce Noto

I've always loved tomatoes. Every year on my birthday, my dad would tell me how my mother had been canning tomatoes right before she went into labor. "That's the reason you love them so much," he'd say. At the end of the story, he'd hand me a bag of tomatoes, knotted at the top in a bow. It was our special tradition.

Not this year, though. Just two months before my birthday, Dad passed away. I told my husband that I didn't even want to see a tomato. Unless they came from Dad, it just wouldn't be the same. Thankfully, only my husband and kids knew about Dad's annual birthday gift and what it meant. I could count on them not to send any tomatoes.

My birthday arrived and I drove myself to school, where I'm a guidance counselor. After a four-hour meeting, I went out for lunch with a friend. It was a good distraction from the sadness I was feeling. On the way back to school, I decided to stop back at my house for a cold drink.

That's when I saw it. A white grocery bag on my front porch, tied at the top in a bow. My heart skipped a beat and tears came to my eyes. Sure enough, when I opened it, I saw that it was full of tomatoes. *I told my family no tomatoes!* I thought, angry. If it wasn't from Dad, it didn't mean anything.

Later, my daughter called. "Mom, I'm so sorry about the tomatoes," she said.

"So you're the one who did that," I said.

"No, Mom, I didn't put them there," she explained. Her husband Travis had received a whole heap of tomatoes from his dad that afternoon. "He knew you liked tomatoes, so he thought of sharing them with you. I had no idea he did until after—he didn't even know it was your birthday."

My daughter apologized again, but I wasn't angry any more. Travis didn't know what the tomatoes meant to me, but Someone did. And He made sure I got my birthday gift, even if my dad couldn't deliver it himself.

HEALING THE PAST

CLAIRE BENSON

I had started burning the October leaves when I heard the telephone ring from the house. It was Mother, calling to say that Harry was ill. Harry was her husband. My stepfather.

"He's got to have surgery, Claire. Won't you come? Won't you be here?"

"He was never there for me," I replied bitterly. "Never in my whole life was he there for me."

"Please," Mother pleaded. "He's in his seventies."

"I'll see," I said.

Back in the yard, I picked up my rake. I scratched its metal prongs along the hard ground, combing mounds of yellow, red, and brown leaves against the fire. In sullen silence I watched them curl and crackle in the path of creeping yellow flames: a flash of red, then charred remains. I thought about Harry, about my hatred for him. About how, despite my knowing better, that hatred had consumed me.

I was five when my own father died. Mother married again when I was eight. Harry was a grass-roots preacher— strong, zealous, and adamant about the ways of the Lord.

His concept of God was one of ruler and judge, and that is what my stepfather became for me.

He allowed no frivolity in the house and little beyond its premises. I never had a birthday party. Until I was seventeen, I was not permitted to date. Then these occasions were carefully monitored, and curfew was 11:00 PM. Card-playing and rock 'n' roll music were forbidden. As a ninth-grader, I made the school cheerleading squad. My stepfather insisted I quit. He frowned upon sports, but one summer afternoon a few neighborhood friends showed me how to play basketball. Secretly I practiced in their backyards. The next fall, I defied my stepfather and qualified for the girls' basketball team. He allowed my playing, but boycotted the games.

All these things I resented, I was missing many activities that were important to me. I was also missing something else. His affection.

As I hung behind Mother's dress among the faithful worshipers who crowded into his church each Sunday, I hungrily watched him clap the shoulders of weathered farmers, shake the hands of calico-clad women, and rustle the hair of towheaded children as they squirmed past.

Oh, that he would touch me that way! If only once, I thought, he would stretch out his hand, call me his child and love me. But he never did.

Now, I was a grown woman with a family of my own. Dan, my husband, would be coming home soon for lunch. The kids would arrive later. I smiled, thinking of how the youngsters hopped off the whining school bus and raced up the drive. It was a ritual. They'd burst through the back door, clamor for a snack, and I'd fix it. Tousling their sandy-brown heads, I'd deal out chocolate chip cookies as they piped like young chicks with news of their day.

Why was my stepfather so cold? For hours as a child I'd imagined him otherwise. The father in my fantasies taught me to swim in the willow-hung lake down the road. He thumped songs from the upright piano in the living room. He pulled me on his lap to read bedtime stories by the light of Mother's favorite globe lamps. My imaginary father loomed large, laughing and kind. The man I called "Dad" was tall and silent and stern.

"Why didn't he ever touch me?" I asked a minister friend of mine years later. "Why couldn't he love me?" Making a tent of his fingers, Dr. McDaniel leaned back in the swivel chair behind his desk. He was silent a long moment. I scanned his paneled office: the familiar picture of Jesus knocking on a door; a large, open Bible, pages ruffled from overuse; the black pulpit robe hung carefully on the wooden coatrack in the corner. How well I knew these things. I had lived with them.

Dr. McDaniel intercepted my glance. A smile danced in the wrinkles around his eyes. "Claire," he said at last, "I know you fairly well. You have high standards. You have a marvelous sensitivity, a caring manner when you talk with others. Where did you get those qualities?"

"I don't know," I blushed. "But anyway, that's not the point."

"I think it's part of the point," Dr. McDaniel persisted.

"What do you mean?"

"I mean that the way we treat others can reflect the way we were treated."

Vehemently, I shook my head. "Not in my case," I said.

"Now, wait a minute," the minister smiled. "Follow along. Has it occurred to you that a parent who didn't care about you would hardly take the time to check you in and out, or monitor your friendships, or insist on high moral standards? Strictness can be lovingness, sometimes."

"Not for Dad," I retorted.

"Maybe not," the minister replied. "But there's something else to consider here. What if your stepfather acted out of fear?"

"Fear?"

"Yes, fear. Didn't you tell me that his own daughter by a previous marriage became pregnant as a teenager? That she ran away from home years before he married your mother?"

"Yes," I mumbled.

"Maybe his fears for you made him harsh."

Dr. McDaniel leaned forward. The chair beneath him squeaked loudly in the silent room. He was composed, kindly. My anger hadn't seemed to unsettle him. My bitterness he acknowledged, but didn't judge. He clasped his hands across the desk between us. His voice was gentle. "When you work through your rage," he said softly, "I think you'll see your stepfather's love for you."

"I don't believe you," I protested. "My stepfather never loved me! He was a hypocrite."

Now, outside, tending the burning leaves, I was so lost in thought that my husband's voice—sudden, close by my shoulder—startled me.

"What's wrong?" he asked.

"It's Dad," I said. "Mother called. He's scheduled for surgery this week. They don't know what's wrong. It could be the end, I suppose."

"How would you feel about that?" Dan asked quietly.

I shrugged and shook my head. "I don't know."

Dan rattled the keys in his pocket as if to delay an awkward beginning. "Claire," he said, shifting his weight, "remember how I felt last year when my father passed on? Remember what you said after his funeral?"

"No." I bit my lip.

"'It's all so temporary.' That's what you said. And you know, Claire, you were right. Today, you have a father. Tomorrow—well…" Dan let the rest evaporate. "Do you think there's any way to heal that relationship?" he asked finally. "I really believe Dr. McDaniel was right when he suggested that your stepfather was thinking of his own daughter when he was so hard on you."

Silence hung heavily between us.

"I'll go in and start the sandwiches for lunch," Dan offered, sensing my sudden need for privacy.

Alone with my thoughts, I looked above the fire to the October sky. So promising. So blue. Such a mismatch with the scorched feeling in my chest. I stared into that boundless blue, and as I did so, something strange happened. Time eclipsed. I saw myself in memory…

A bashful teenager, small for my age, wanting so desperately to please my stepfather, never understanding why he rejected me so, I stood, trembling before him. It was my senior year, and I was home from a date at 11:20 PM, twenty minutes late. The delay was unavoidable, and I tried to explain. He wouldn't listen. He roared unfairly, "What kind of standards do you set for yourself, Claire?"

But as I looked further, and saw beyond the pain the memory caused, I gazed upon my stepfather's customary black suit—stiff, formidable, but the cuffs were worn and frayed, the elbows shiny. He had often denied himself to provide for us. I saw his grim face. Yet there was worry and fear in his eyes. Before I had seen only rage.

My vision, like the cloud-free sky, became unaccountably clear. All at once I was seeing his temper, his rigidity, his suspicions, as symptoms—symptoms of hurts within himself and concern for me.

Dan's parting question about healing the relationship came back to me now, mingled with Dr. McDaniel's words. What had the minister said?

When you heal the relationship, you heal the past. Forgiveness is a gift to the one who forgives. Jesus knew that. That's why He urged us to forgive.

Suddenly, without warning, something snapped inside, releasing the tears. Tears long held at bay.

"Oh, God," I anguished, "listen to Your forgotten child, Claire. Can I forgive that man? Can I ever forgive my stepfather? How many times do You forgive?"

"Seventy times seven," Jesus told His disciple Peter.

"He's in his seventies," Mother had said.

"Someday you'll face the past and forgive," Dr. McDaniel had told me.

Weeping still, I gripped the rake. I pushed a few stray leaves toward the fire. The towering mound had condensed quietly into settled black ash. Like burned-out rage, the flames were spent. I scraped the hot remains together. Then, unraveling the garden hose, I soaked the embers cold.

The water was cool, inviting. Impulsively I splashed my face. Then resolutely I shook my head. I strode into the house.

"I'm going home," I told Dan. "You know," I swallowed, "I need to be able to love him. I need to love Dad. If I catch a flight out this afternoon, could you and the kids drive me to the airport?"

Sunset ribbons streaked the sky burnt orange as my plane settled in the blue-hazed hills of North Carolina. Then, once again, I was there—in my stepfather's house. It seemed smaller in a way. I hugged Mother, then stepped into the living room. Her favorite glass lamps, the ballooning shape of Victorian fashion, threw iridescent pink across pale green walls. Carved, wooden knickknacks—homey, inexpensive—crowded the top of the upright piano. A hymnal lay open above the silent keys. I walked slowly across the floor. Memories swirled ghostlike in my path.

When you heal the relationship, you heal the past....

Down the hall, Dad's bedroom door stood open.

I paused in the rectangle of yellow light that stretched from the doorway to his tall, four-poster bed. The window on the other side was open. Dad lay there, tired eyes scanning the autumn evening. His fingers stroked the white, tufted spread, I looked at his hands—those hands that had given countless congregations God's blessing. Sensing my presence, Dad turned his head. He was surprised, I could tell, that I had come.

I faltered a moment, the grown-up woman wrestling with the child inside. He cleared a rasping throat.

"I wish," he struggled in a hoarse whisper, "I wish I had been more—more…"

"I know," I said simply.

A smile relaxed his face. "Come close, daughter," he said. Then at last, at long last, he stretched out his hand. God's healing was in his touch.

THE CARD

PAT FRANTZ CERCONE

Every year in May, my father finds in his mailbox a Mother's Day card from his only child. This may seem strange, but it's perfectly natural to honor the man who's been the only mother I've had for more than thirty years.

He's the one who taught me how to make homemade stuffing, successfully sew a zipper into a pair of pants, and combine just the right amount of flour and egg yolks to make noodles. That may not seem so unusual these days, when men are more sensitive and flexible. But my dad took over mom-duty when my mother died in 1974, well before the movie *Mr. Mom* made grocery-shopping, bread-baking, laundry-doing dads cool. And he took his mom role seriously.

When I was getting ready to graduate elementary school, my friends' mothers took them shopping for new dresses. My dad went to the fabric store and bought a pattern, shimmering material, and sewing doodads, and then spent several hours huddled over the sewing machine to make a beautiful dress for me. When I was having trouble in sewing class making a pair of shorts, he not only helped me finish them but also made me a week's worth of shorts in bicentennial material so I looked really hip during the summer of 1976.

When I needed to take a treat to my school's bake sale, Dad headed to the kitchen, grabbed a tin of Hershey's cocoa, and baked a pan of brownies. His ego was boosted when those brownies were the first to sell out.

None of this was a threat to his manhood, even though men at that time were often judged by how cool they looked in their leisure suits or how well they danced the hustle. His self-esteem was strengthened when, at sleepovers, I would model the flannel pajamas he made for me. He enjoyed the flabbergasted looks when he gave people gifts of homemade preserves.

Dad did all this while he worked full time, ran a household, and raised a daughter alone.

So each year, as I struggle to find the perfect Mother's Day card for him, it would be easier to forget it. After all, Father's Day is just a month later, right? *Au contraire.* One year I neglected to send a Mother's Day card, and I still hear about it. My father often says he's more proud of what he accomplished as my mother than as my father because being a mother was so much harder.

But if you think that means I can forget him on Father's Day…

AL'S USED CARS
LONNIE HULL DUPONT

My stepfather came into my life when I was five years old. My eight-year-old sister and I were sitting on the floor watching television when a tall, good-looking man with a Clark Gable mustache and dark wavy hair walked in the front door. He paused, looked down at us, and smiled a lopsided grin. When I asked him what his name was, he said it was Joe. Then he winked.

His name was actually Al, but my sister and I called him Joe until he married our mother a few months later. Once he moved into the house as our stepfather, we girls decided on our own to call him Dad.

I was so glad to have this new Dad. I adored him. He was a little older than the fathers of my friends, and he was about the most exotic-looking man I ever saw among them. I recall having a friend over who stopped in her tracks when she saw Dad reading the paper in his black pajamas and red plaid smoking jacket. My little friend stared at him and said, "That's your *dad*?" My mother was a beautiful woman, and watching the two of them dance to Nat King Cole singing "Rambling Rose" was something wonderful to behold.

Dad was a man who never met a stranger. His friendly "Come on in and sit a spell..." to houseguests was as predictable as his eventually taking all visiting men to his barn to look over whatever machinery was out there. He told great stories and had a wisecracking sense of humor, but he also had impeccable manners.

And he loved cars. We lived in rural southeastern Michigan, which meant we lived in the shadow of the auto industry. Everyone was nuts about cars when I was growing up, and apparently this was true when Dad was growing up, too, because he bought his first car when he was only thirteen. It was a Model-T, paid for with a box of chickens.

In my growing-up years, Dad bought a different car every few months, sometimes more than one, trading in whatever he had for something different. Sunday drives for our family meant trolling for used cars. I mean, the man loved automobiles, all kinds, and he loved to tinker with them. Any vehicle ran like a top once he got his hands on it. His advice to me was that I should never buy a car new—"Give it a year to find the kinks," he'd say. For a hobby, he'd buy cars that didn't run, get them going, clean them up, then park them at the roadside to sell for a little extra cash. Since he also loved to maintain a beautiful lawn, things never looked trashy when he sold a car. Nevertheless, we jokingly called our place Al's Used Cars.

Dad was one of the most generous people I've ever met. He worked hard and made a good living, and he shared what he had. He didn't simply pick up a tab; when it came to cars, he shared the wealth there as well. I learned to drive at age eleven, and at age fifteen I was given my first car—a used, three-speed Corvair that I drove in the fields until I could legally drive on the road.

And while it was true that anyone who lived with Dad always had wheels, it could be true for those who didn't live with him as well. My cousin who wasn't even related to Dad had an important date for the prom—he would marry his date a few years later—but he didn't have much else. Dad grew up poor, and he understood. He handed the keys to his own shiny black Lincoln to my cousin for the evening. Believe me, that cousin never forgot.

A new family moved in down the road from us, and we didn't actually know them. But we heard that their child had a serious accident with their lawn mower. Her injury required a long hospitalization at a university hospital, a two-hour round trip from home. People didn't drive long commutes back then, and there was no hospital housing for families, so that drive would be especially problematic for her parents who didn't have a second car.

No worries. If your neighbor is Al, you have a car. When Dad heard about their situation, he came to the rescue in the best way he knew. He drove one of the many cars he tinkered with to their house and told them to drive it until their child was out of the hospital. Then he walked back home.

But as time wore on, Dad had some personal problems. I never really knew what was going on inside him. He kept his problems to himself, and that stoicism caused him to become very quiet. He still had a heart of gold, and he still was jovial with strangers. But at home, he was tense and seemed unable to relax. One way he dealt with his anxiety was to keep working on cars. But he also became almost silent for many years. I didn't understand it when I was growing up. I had been so thrilled to have this new father the first few years he was with us. What happened to him?

For many years, Dad and I barely spoke to each other. We weren't angry with each other. It was simply that he had withdrawn for reasons that had nothing to do with me. But I didn't know that. I assumed he didn't love me.

Now that I'm older, I understand a lot that I didn't understand in my youth. One of the most important things I've learned is that not everyone can express love in obvious ways, and Dad was one of those people. Even before he became quiet, he would never reach out and hug. He seldom praised or made any comment one way or another about my accomplishments or behavior.

He never said, "I love you," except once when he was heavily medicated on his way to a surgery.

But I always had a car. Dad provided me with wheels all through my later high school years and even through six years of college. If my car had trouble, he fixed it. If I had a fender-bender, he fixed it. I never picked out my own cars, even the ones I bought myself, until I was thirty years old and moved out of state. He did it. I was happy he would do it, and I took it for granted. And what I didn't realize until much later was that this was how Dad showed his love for me. He gave freely of the one solid thing he truly knew and understood, even when life confused him—cars.

Dad lived to be fairly old. My husband and I had just returned from visiting my folks in Florida when we got the call that Dad was in the hospital. I was about to leave on a business trip, so my sister agreed to fly down to Florida and keep me posted.

In actuality, Dad was dying. He went into a short coma, then pulled out for his last night alive. My sister and mother were with him as he sat up and had coffee and a snack. When they checked to see how mentally aware he was, he named who was with him in the room. He thought I was there too. But I was in a Nashville hotel room, nauseated and unable to rest, just as he lay dying. Soon after I finally went to sleep, I got the call that he'd passed away. I like to think that God graciously put Dad and me in touch long-distance that last night.

A few years later, I was talking to an old friend of mine who grew up in Ohio. When we were in high school and college, I used to drive the ninety-minute drive to her family's house for visits since I always had wheels. And before I'd drive back to Michigan, her dad always checked my car over. He'd pop the hood, check the tires, and call it good. This was the same thing he did for his daughter.

After my friend's father died, she and I talked about him and decided that he expressed his affection by doing the things that kept his daughter—and her friend—safe, like checking the car over. This was how both our dads showed their love. They kept our cars running.

Today I am fortunate to have a good husband. I'm also fortunate that he takes care of my car. He checks fluids and tires regularly, and while sometimes I might not think it's necessary, I never say so. I no longer take such things for granted. Thanks to my stepfather—a man who stepped up to the job of fathering in the only way he could—I know my husband is showing me in a very sweet and concrete way that he loves me.

Life Lessons

One night a father overheard
his son pray:

Dear God, make me
the kind of man my daddy is.

Later that night, the father prayed,

Dear God, make me the kind of man
my son wants me to be.

~ Author Unknown

IT'S A START

GARY SMALLEY AND JOHN TRENT

We know a wealthy couple in Dallas who have really struggled with teaching their children servanthood. For one thing the kids have had almost whatever they've wanted for years. They've become so accustomed to others meeting their needs that the idea of "serving" sounded like something from the Middle Ages...or Mars.

The father in that family realized he was getting a late start, but hey, it was better than no start at all!

A week or so before the holidays, he said to his family, "We're going to do something different this Thanksgiving."

His teenagers sat up and listened. Usually when he said things like that it meant something exotic. Like parasailing in the Bahamas.

But not this time. "We're going to go down to the mission," he told them, "and we're going to serve Thanksgiving dinner to some poor and homeless people."

"We're going to do *what*?"

"Come on, Dad, you're kidding...aren't you? Tell us you're kidding."

He wasn't. They went along with it because of his firm insistence, but no one was happy about it. For some reason their dad had "gotten weird" and apparently it was something he just had to get out of his system. Serving at the mission! What if their friends heard about it?

No one could have predicted what happened that day. And no one in the family could remember when they had had a better time together. They hustled around the kitchen, dished up turkey and dressing, sliced pumpkin pie, and refilled countless coffee cups. They clowned around with the little kids and listened to old folks tell stories of Thanksgivings long ago and far away.

The dad of the family was thoroughly pleased (would you believe stunned?) by the way his kids responded. But nothing could have prepared him for their request a few weeks later.

"Dad...we want to go back to the mission and serve Christmas dinner!"

And they did. As the kids hoped, they met some of the same people they'd become acquainted with at Thanksgiving. One needy family in particular had been on their minds, and they all lit up when they saw them back in the chow line again. Since that time, the family has had several contacts. The pampered teenagers have rolled up their sleeves more than once to serve the families from one of Dallas' poorer neighborhoods.

There was a marked but subtle change in that home. The kids didn't seem to be taking things for granted anymore. Their parents found them more serious…more responsible. Yes, it was a late start. But it was a start.

IS IT THE TRUTH?

LESLIE E. DUNCAN

I shall never forget that short question my father asked me as soon as we were alone in his study. His eyes were watching me closely. They were searching eyes rather than sharp, condemning ones. He was looking for the truth from his son, who had done something seriously wrong. If he had heard what I'd done, he would punish me for it.

I puzzled to myself for a brief moment whether I should deny having done it and trust to luck that he would believe me rather than the other people, or should I come right out with the truth.

"Is it true?" he repeated.

I detected appealing love in the tone of his voice rather than stern judgment. He was talking to me as man-to-man though we were quite different in our ages. I blinked my eyes hesitantly for only a split second more.

"Yes, Dad!" I almost smiled in reply from the relief it was to me. "It is true! I did it!"

I did not have long to wait to know what he was going to do about the wrong. How much he wanted us children to grow up to be fine Christian people. I was breathing more easily already, but the uncertainty had not been cleared yet.

"Son," he began, as his right hand was extended toward mine and his left hand was placed on my shoulder, "I'm proud of you!"

The tears that welled up in his eyes assured me he meant every word of what he said. I wondered at first what it all signified. Here I had done what I knew was against my father's wishes. He had heard about it, and I had acknowledged my guilt. Then he declared he was proud of me. That did not sound like my minister father.

"I'm proud of you," he repeated and explained, "to know that you had the courage to tell the truth, even though you thought you would be punished for what you'd done."

My eyes opened wider. I was seeing something I hadn't noticed so clearly before. For one thing, I saw what stood well to the front—if not clear out ahead of everything else—in my father's estimation. Through the eyes of his thoughts I was seeing too a new idea of character values. "Is it true?" had a greater importance than a demanding "What have you done?"

He explained in more detail that he wanted us to tell the truth at all times, no matter what it might cost us. He assured me that as far as punishment was concerned, he would punish us more for telling an untruth to cover something wrong than for telling the truth.

I felt better at once when I told the truth. I could think more clearly about the problem waiting to be solved. Dad had not taken care of that for the two of us. I wondered what to expect next. I certainly had been surprised. I saw everything differently.

"I want you to tell me the truth now," he continued, "the way you just did in such a fine way."

"What?" I asked, a bit puzzled.

He wanted to know if I thought I had done what was right. I was in no mood at all to deny this. Why should I? I told the truth before, so I would do it now too. I assured him I was sure I had done wrong and that I should not have done it.

"What do you think you should do to let people know, especially those you have not done right to, that you are sorry and will not do it again?" he asked.

I was busy thinking. Finally I thought of how I could let them know I was really sorry. In addition to that I knew how I could undo some of what had been done; I could remove some of the damage.

"One more thing, Son," smiled Dad with increasing pride.

I wondered what else he could think of before I would leave his study. So much had happened already in our talk together.

"How are you going to make sure you will remember not to do it the next time?" he questioned. "That is what punishment is for—to make us really sorry for what we have done and to be sure we will remember not to do it again."

I outlined roughly what I thought would be suitable for this. He listened closely.

"Since you had the courage to tell the truth," he suggested, "how would this suit you?" He modified the punishment I had suggested for myself. He was not excusing me from the guilt of doing something quite wrong. He was rewarding me in a wise way for being completely truthful about it.

"Before we leave the room," he concluded, "let's kneel right here and tell God all about what has happened. We can ask Him to help us so that we will not make the same or a similar mistake again. God knows the pleasant truth is much better than any unpleasant truth. He can help us so that we will always have the pleasant truth from our daily thoughts and actions."

On our knees together, my wonderful father had one of his informal prayer talks with God about our situation—not just mine. I asked God in my childlike way for forgiveness for what I had done and for strength to avoid doing it again.

From that day to the time of his death many years later, I never was afraid to tell my father the whole truth. In fact, I thought so much of him and his respect for the truth that I was always ashamed not to tell him the truth—every bit of it.

My Father's Gift

Kazuko Kay Nakao

The strawberries were blooming when the soldiers arrived in trucks. It was March, one month before berries usually appeared on my father's farm. But that year, 1942, spring came early to the Pacific Northwest, and every row of our fifteen acres was speckled with white and yellow blossoms. It would have been a record crop. But we never got to pick it. My family is Japanese, and days earlier notices had appeared on telephone poles around our small island in the Puget Sound: "INSTRUCTIONS TO ALL JAPANESE Living on Bainbridge Island: All Japanese persons, both alien and non-alien, will be evacuated from this area by twelve noon, Monday, March 30, 1942." It didn't matter that my parents had lived in America since 1918, or that my father, shortly after Pearl Harbor was bombed, had cashed in his life insurance and used the money to buy liberty bonds. The soldiers, carrying guns with bayonets, loaded us into green army trucks and drove us to a ferry terminal, where the island's other Japanese families had been gathered. We were each allowed one suitcase and whatever we could carry in our arms. I packed a photo album. It wasn't much to remember twenty-two years of life. But I didn't know if I would ever see my friends again. I didn't want to forget what they looked like.

I am one of 120,000 Japanese-Americans who were interned for three and a half years in prison camps during World War II. All of those people went to the camps as my family did: forced from their homes by soldiers and taken on buses and trains to live in tar-paper barracks far from any city, in remote places like the Arizona desert and Heart Mountain, Wyoming. When my family arrived at Manzanar, a camp for ten thousand Japanese on the alkali plains of California's dry Owens Valley, my heart broke. The camp was desolate, a shocking contrast to the lush evergreens and foggy damp of Bainbridge Island. Sand storms blew grit into our hair and teeth. Guards raked searchlights past the barracks at night. Even after transferring eleven months later to a similarly sized camp in Minidoka, Idaho, where the summers weren't so hot, I couldn't accept that we were in prison. My parents were kind, honest people. My younger brother and four younger sisters and I were farm kids—we rarely even left Bainbridge Island, except to shop for school clothes in Seattle. We had done nothing wrong! And yet there we were, surrounded by barbed wire and assigned to one twenty-foot-by-sixteen-foot room with army cots, hanging-blanket partitions as closets, and an oil-burning stove, our only warmth when winter temperatures plunged to twenty degrees below zero.

It wasn't just the hardship—I was used to that on a farm. It was seeing my father stripped of everything he had. He was a quiet, dignified man who wore suits when his photograph was taken and helped to arrange marriage introductions on our island. He had saved his money for years to buy our land, then cleared the fields of rocks and trees by hand and built a white farmhouse with six bedrooms, a modern kitchen, and even a washing machine, so my mother no longer had to scrub our clothes.

But none of that mattered when, a few weeks before the soldiers took us away, FBI agents barged into our house, arrested my father, and accused my mother of hiding a short-wave radio in the living room. The accusation was false, of course, and the agents pressed no charges, releasing my father that evening. But I had never seen him so frightened. He told us to make a pile of everything Japanese we owned—books, records, scrolls, toys, gifts from relatives. Then he burned them. I watched the flames rise in the farmyard, wondering if we would ever feel safe again.

A month after arriving at Minidoka, I married a man I had been dating back home—Isami Nakao, a strawberry farmer also imprisoned. Our wedding was in Twin Falls, eighteen miles away. We had to get a day pass from guards, take a bus, and wander the streets until we found a minister who would marry us. Sometime later we received a letter from the manager of Isami's farm. The man warned that if Isami wanted his land back, he would have to pay—more than we could afford. We talked to lawyers at the camp. But they could do nothing. And so we were forced to sell all sixty of Isami's acres, his house, and his equipment for ten thousand dollars—far less than they were worth. Isami spoke little about the sale. But I ached to see him lose his livelihood. He had built the house on that farm just six months before the soldiers came.

Finally the war ended and Minidoka closed in 1945, dissolving as quickly as it had risen. We returned to Bainbridge Island filled with apprehension. I worried that my father's farm would also be taken away. That my friends would refuse to speak to me. That no one would give us jobs. But I thanked God that at least we were free.

My fears proved unfounded. My friends were happy to see me, and the manager of my father's farm returned it to him graciously. There was only one problem. The widow who had been renting our house refused to move out—even though she hadn't sent us a check in years. "I used the money for repairs," she said brusquely.

"What repairs?" my father asked.

"Many things," she said, and slammed the door.

"What do we do now?" Mom asked.

"We move into the basement," my father said. Everyone unloaded the car and stood in the dank, dark room, looking at each other. After a time, a sly smile spread across my father's face. "Let's prepare some fish and pickled daikon," he said. Pickled daikon smells like Limburger cheese, and soon that aroma was wafting through the floorboards.

The widow moved out.

Other Japanese were not so fortunate. Many lost everything. And so, in those initial years back home, we kept our heads down, said nothing about the camps, and threw ourselves into every American activity we could find. Isami and I got jobs at the local Town and Country Market—me as a checker, Isami as a meat cutter (he had worked at the Manzanar meat warehouse). We had three children, and I signed them up for Brownies, Cub Scouts, and sports. When Isami and I bought a house on a small rise overlooking the Puget Sound, I brought to it only a few mementos of our past, including a doll dressed in a blue and orange kimono sent by my grandmother from Japan in 1930. It had been one of my favorite dolls and had escaped the bonfire of our Japanese things only because we had packed it away when I was a teenager and forgotten it in the rush. I was so glad to find it. My grandmother had perished when the atom bomb fell on Hiroshima.

Two years after we returned from the camps, men from the local school district came to my father and asked to buy part of his farm. They needed land for a new school. I wondered what he would say. That farm meant everything to him. He thought about their request for several days. Then, one evening, when Isami and I were at his house, he sat down at the dinner table and said, "I am going to sell to the district. And I am going to sell for what I paid for the land, not for what it is worth today."

My eyes widened. It was an extraordinary act of generosity—especially after all we had been through. "Why, father?" I asked.

"Because, Kazuko, this country has given me everything I have," he said, using my Japanese name. "I came here with nothing. And now look. I have six children, all educated—for free! The best education in the world. What other country would do that? Listen, Kazuko. We must be good citizens here, no matter what happened. Study hard, contribute to our community, and look forward, not back."

I didn't think much about those words in the years that followed. They were so typical of my father, and I mostly remembered them when encouraging my own kids to do their homework. It wasn't until recently, when I opened the local newspaper and saw his name in an article, that I truly understood what my father had been trying to tell me. The article reported that the island school district had chosen to name its newest school Sonoji Sakai Intermediate School— after my father. I had to set the paper down and catch my breath. Our local Japanese club had put his name forward several months before as a prominent early member of the community. But the district was considering eighty-four nominations from all over the island, and I had assumed the school would be named after an important figure in Washington history. And yet there it was: my father's name on a school for six hundred fifth and sixth graders. The name, said the article, would honor all Bainbridge Island *issei*, the Japanese word for first-generation immigrants. I thought of my father coming to America, working hard, enduring humiliation in the camps, and finally offering generosity to the nation that had imprisoned him. Look forward, not back. It was, I realized, a lesson in healing, in forgiveness, in refusing to drink from the cup of bitterness.

Not long ago I was walking the halls at Sakai School, where an etching of my parents fills a window beside the entrance, and the staff has designed a curriculum for teaching students about the Japanese internment. I was on the bottom floor, where, along one wall, teachers have erected a timeline of the internment and tacked up documents from that era, including the poster that told us, all those years ago, that we had to leave our island home. Near the poster was a glass case enclosing a doll—a doll with a blue and orange kimono, the doll my grandmother had given me. I looked at the doll for awhile and thought about how it had nearly missed being destroyed in that bonfire of our Japanese things. Now it was my gift to this school where children will never forget that, once, Japanese-Americans were taken from their homes and put in prisons far away. I reached out and touched the glass. Then I turned away and walked back down the hall, out into the cool, moist air of Bainbridge Island. That air so good for growing strawberries. So good for calling home.

A Lesson from the Mound

Beth Mullally

My father was always the pitcher in our backyard baseball games. He got this honor in part because my sister, brother, and I couldn't get the ball over home plate, but also because, with one wooden leg, running after a fly ball that got hit into the cornfield out back just wasn't his strong suit. And so he'd stand under the hot sun, pitching endlessly while we took turns at bat.

He ran our games with the authority of a Yankees manager. He was boss, and he had requirements. We had to chatter in the outfield, for one. I must have said, "Nobatternobatternobatternobatter" five thousand times while growing up. And we had to try to outrun the ball, no matter how futile it might seem. This was baseball, by golly, and there was only one way to play: the way the Yankees played.

Going up to bat against my father was not easy. None of this self-esteem stuff for him, trying to make a kid feel good about hitting a ball that's standing still. He was never the least bit sorry when he struck me out, and he did it all the time.

"Do you want to play ball or don't you?" he'd ask if I began whining about his fast pitches.

I wanted to. And when I'd finally connect with the ball—oh man, I knew I deserved the hit. I'd be grinning all the way down the first-base line.

I'd turn to look at my father on the pitcher's mound. He'd take off his glove and tuck it under his arm, and then clap for me. To my ears, it sounded like a standing ovation at Yankee stadium.

Years later, my son was to learn these same rules about baseball from my father. By then, though, Dad was pitching from a wheelchair. In some medical fluke, he had lost his other leg.

But nothing else had changed. My boy was required to chatter from the outfield. He had to try outrunning the ball, no matter how futile it might seem. And when he whined that the pitch was too fast, he got the ultimatum: "Do you want to play ball or don't you?"

He did.

My boy was nine years old the spring before his grandfather died. They played a lot of ball that season, and there was the usual litany of complaints that my father was pitching too hard.

"Just keep your eye on the ball!" Dad would holler at him.

Finally, at one at-bat, he did. He swung and connected dead-center. The ball slammed down the middle, straight at my father.

He reached for it, but missed. And in the process, his wheelchair tilted backward. In ever such slow motion, we watched him and his chair topple until he came down on his back with a thud.

My boy stood stock-still halfway to first.

"You don't ever stop running!" my father roared from the ground. "The ball's still in play! You run!"

When my boy stood safe at first base, he turned to look at my father lying on his back on the pitcher's mound. He saw him take off his glove and tuck it under his arm. And then he heard his grandfather clap for him.

Asking for Forgiveness
Luis Palau

When I returned from a trip overseas, I sensed that something was wrong between Keith, one of our twins, and me. So I asked him, "Keith, have I done anything that really hurt your feelings?"

Instantly, he said, "Yes. Last Christmas you promised me a special toy that I really wanted and you never gave it to me."

The fact is that I'd completely forgotten about it. I probed further. "Is there anything else hurtful to you I've done for which I've never asked for your forgiveness?"

Again, his answer was immediate: "Remember when Mom said you had to go to the hospital because Stephen was going to be born? You left us at home and took off in a hurry. Remember?" I did.

"Well, you took off and forgot the suitcase with all the stuff." I couldn't believe all the details he remembered! "After you left Mom at the hospital, you came back and you were huffy. When you got here, the suitcase had been opened and everything was thrown all over the place. And you punished me."

My heart sank. "And you didn't do it?" I asked.

"No, I didn't."

I felt terrible. I hugged Keith and asked him to forgive me. There was an instant improvement in our relationship after that. But his honesty made me think of our other son, Kevin. After all, maybe I'd hurt him too. I went to find Kevin and I asked him the same question: "Have I ever done something wrong and never asked your forgiveness or promised you something and never kept my promise?"

Kevin's answer was as instant as his brother's had been. "Last Christmas you promised us a special toy and you never bought it for us." Kevin had no idea I'd just talked to Keith about the same thing.

Though it was way past Christmas, I took my two sons to the store that day and bought them what I had promised. The important thing wasn't the toy that was all the rage at the time. Obviously, it was a big deal to my boys even if it wasn't to me. The problem was I'd made a promise all too lightly and dropped the ball as their father.

At times, trying to fulfill all my obligations and responsibilities as a husband and father and an evangelist seems impossible. So often, an excruciating schedule lies before me, and sometimes I'm gone from home for weeks at a time. But I listened to my sons and I learned that keeping my word is one of the most important things I can do—no matter what my schedule says.

WAKE-UP CALL

BOB WELCH

I was sitting in a bathtub full of moldy sheetrock when my thirteen-year-old son asked the question. "Can you take me golfing sometime?" I had a bathroom to remodel. It was fall, and the forecast for the next week was for a one hundred percent chance of Oregon's liquid sunshine. I wanted to say no. "Sure," I said. "What did you have in mind?"

"Well, maybe you could, like, pick up Jared and me after school on Friday and take us out to Oakway."

"Sounds good."

Friday came. The showers continued. Looking out the window, moldy sheetrock seemed the saner choice. But at the appointed hour, I changed from home-improvement garb to rain-protection garb and loaded the boys' clubs and mine in the back of the car. In front of the school, Ryan and Jared piled in. Ryan looked at me with a perplexed expression.

"What's with the golf hat, Dad?" he said.

What a silly question, I thought. *It was like asking a scuba diver what's with the swim fins.*

"Well, I thought we were going to play some golf."

A peculiar pause ensued, like a phone line temporarily gone dead.

"Uh, you're going *too*?" he asked.

Suddenly, it struck me like a three-iron to my gut. I hadn't been invited.

Thirteen years of parenting flashed before my eyes. The birth. The diapers. The late-night feedings. Helping with homework. Building forts. Fixing bikes. Going to games. Going camping. Going everywhere together—my son and me.

Now I hadn't been invited. This was it. This was the end of our relationship as I had always known it. This was "Adios, Old Man, thanks for the memories but I'm old enough to swing my own clubs now, so go back to your rocking chair and crossword puzzles and—oh yeah—here's a half-off coupon for your next bottle of Geritol."

All these memories sped by in about two seconds, leaving me three seconds to respond before Ryan would get suspicious and think I had actually expected to be playing golf with him and his friend.

I had to say something. I wanted to say this: *How could you do this to me? Throw me overboard like unused crab bait?* We had always been a team. But this was abandonment. Adult abuse!

This was Lewis turning to Clark in 1805 and saying: "Later, Bill. I can make it the rest of the way to Oregon without you." John Glenn radioing Mission Control to say, thanks, but he could take it from here. Simon bailing out on Garfunkel during "Bridge Over Troubled Water." (Okay, that did happen, but much later.)

Why did it all have to change?

Enough of this mind-wandering. I needed to level with him. I needed to express how hurt I was. Share my gut-level feelings. Muster all the courage I could find, bite the bullet, and spill my soul.

So I said, "Me? Play? Naw. You know I'm up to my ears in the remodel project."

We drove on in silence for a few moments. "So, how are you planning to pay for this?" I asked, my wounded ego reaching for the dagger.

"Uh, could you lend me seven dollars?"

Oh, I get it. He doesn't want *me*, but he'll gladly take my money.

"No problem," I said.

I dropped him and Jared off, wished them luck, and headed for home. My son was on his own now. Nobody there to tell him how to fade a five-iron, how to play that tricky downhiller, how to hit the sand shot. And what if there's lightening? What about hypothermia? A runaway golf cart? A band of militant gophers? He's so small. Who would take care of him?

There I was, alone, driving away from him. Not just for now. Forever. This was it. The bond was broken. Life would never be the same.

I walked in the door. "What are you doing home?" my wife asked.

I knew it would sound like some thirteen-year-old who was the only one in the gang not invited to the slumber party, but maintaining my immature demure, I said it anyway.

"I wasn't *invited*," I replied, with a trace of snottiness.

Another one of those peculiar pauses ensued. Then my wife laughed. Out loud. At first I was hurt. Then I, too, laughed, the situation suddenly becoming much clearer.

I went back to the bathroom remodel and began realizing that this is what life is all about: change. This is what father and sons must ultimately do: change. This is what I've been preparing him for since he first looked at me and screamed in terror: not to play golf without me, but to take on the world without me. With his own set of clubs. His own game plan. His own faith.

God was remodeling my son. Adding some space here. Putting in a new feature there. In short, allowing him to become more than he could ever be if I continued to hover over him. Just like when I was a kid and, at Ryan's age, I would sling my plaid golf bag over my shoulder and ride my bike five miles across town to play golf at a small public course called Marysville that I imagined as Augusta National.

I remember how grown-up I felt, walking into that dark clubhouse, the smoke rising from the poker game off to the left and proudly plunking down my two dollars for nine holes. Would I have wanted my father there with me that day? Naw. A boy's gotta do what a boy's gotta do: grow up.

I went back to the bathroom remodel project. A few hours later I heard Ryan walk in the front door. I heard him complain to his mother that his putts wouldn't drop, that his drives were slicing, and that the course was like a lake. He sounded like someone I knew. His tennis shoes squeaked with water as I heard him walk back to where I was working on the bathroom.

"Dad," he said, dripping on the floor, "my game stinks. Can you take me golfing sometime? I need your help."

I wanted to hug him. Rev my radial-arm saw in celebration. Shout: "I'm still needed!" I wanted to tell God, "Thanks for letting me be part of this kid's remodel job."

Instead, I got one of those serious-dad looks on my face and stoically said, "Sure, Ry, anytime."

WHERE ARE YOU PADDLING?

GEORGE WALTHER

I'm a single dad, raising my daughter as her custodial parent (her mother lives in Canada), so these times we share together are especially memorable. My daughter Kelcie was in kindergarten when she taught me my biggest lesson about navigating through life. It happened when our YMCA father-daughter "Indian Princess" tribe went on a campout and we shared our first canoeing experience. Kelcie gleefully ran to the lakeshore, climbed in front with her paddle, and I settled into the stern with mine. Five other father-daughter canoe teams pushed off at the same time.

The others paddled in different directions with varying degrees of swiftness toward the neighboring camp on the far shore, the intriguing inlet to the south or north toward a lakeshore cabin. Kelcie and I barely made any headway at all.

As a professional speaker who is always eager to educate, I presented Kelcie with a highly customized fatherly seminar on the theory of canoe physics. While stroking with my own paddle to balance her tentative strokes, all of which were on the right side of the boat, I patiently explained how one should paddle.

"Stop paddling, Dad! I want to do it myself."

"But, honey, you're only paddling on the right side, and that's why we're curving to the left and hardly making any progress. Look how fast Jeff and Jessica are moving. They're paddling on both sides of their boat and they're already halfway to the cove. Now I'll paddle on the left back here to balance your strokes on the right. You see?"

"No! I want to do it my way."

"Sweetheart, if we don't paddle together and you just stroke on the right, we'll go in one big circle and we'll never get to the cove or the inlet, or the boat wreck, or anywhere. You do want to get somewhere, don't you? We're already way behind the others."

"I don't care. I want to do all the paddling myself."

I, the expert on all things, saw Dave and Susie's canoe already nearing the distant inlet, and Jeff and Jessica had almost reached the cove. Their wakes showed that their courses were mostly straight and true. When my daughter wasn't looking, I furtively stroked my paddle on the left side to straighten our course.

Kelcie caught me. She whipped around and shot me a defiant look: "Dad, stop it! I want to paddle on my own."

My instant seminar had not impressed her. No hint of applause. "You'll see. We'll be far behind all the other canoes. They'll be having fun at the cove, and we will have gone nowhere but in one big circle." I sat back sullenly, annoyed that my child was ignoring my excellent, wise advice. I abandoned my "let's get somewhere" strategy and let Kelcie paddle her own way. Sure enough, we slowly arced in one big lazy circle. And, as I leaned back in the stern with the paddle in my lap, I realized I was enjoying the view much more than if we had been making straight, swift progress toward a destination. Kelcie was happy, and I was too.

That's how she taught me that the goal of father-daughter canoeing is not to reach a destination swiftly; it's to enjoy being together and to relish where you are while respecting others' wishes and learning a little something. And isn't that also the goal of life?

The lesson in the canoe helped me to determine the direction for my own life. Giving a thousand talks, making X million dollars, or being featured on some TV show is not really that important in the scheme of things. My uppermost goal is to raise a loving, happy child with whom I enjoy life. Here's how I pull it off. When I first became a single parent, I closed my big impressive downtown office and added office space to my home. I get up very early between four and five, and work in my home office until seven. From seven until nine, I'm on dad duty with Kelcie. After breakfast and schoolwork together, I walk my daughter to the bus stop and chat with the other parents and kids. When the bus pulls away, I return to my office. At 3:44 PM, I walk to the bus stop and welcome my child home. I don't work in the evening, I parent.

My days are now more balanced, and I know I can spend more time on work later in my career. I'm content to have a comfortable life; I don't want a yacht or a mansion. Because of my priorities, my clients can count on having a happy, healthy, sane person show up in front of their audiences. And most important of all, my daughter and I both benefit from having a satisfying, loving relationship.

Knowing where I'm paddling makes the journey all the more joyful.

(Acknowledgments continued from page iv)

"Benched" by James Robison is reprinted from *My Father's Face: Entrusting Our Lives to a God Who Loves Us,* copyright © 1997 by James Robison. Used by permission of WaterBrook Multnomah, an imprint of Crown Publishing Group, a division of Random House, Inc.

"The Card" by Pat Frantz Cercone copyright © 2006 by Pat Frantz Cercone, is reprinted from *Wisdom of Our Fathers* by Tim Russert. Used by permission of Random House, Inc.

"The Companion" by Beth Hackett is copyright © 2006 by Pat Frantz Cercone, from *Wisdom of Our Fathers* by Tim Russert. Used by permission of Random House, Inc.

"Dad's Mark" by Bill Hybels is from *Honest to God?* Copyright © 1990 by Bill Hybels. Published by Zondervan Publishing.

"Driving Lessons" by Charles Swindoll is reprinted by permission from *The Grace Awakening,* 1990, Thomas Nelson, Inc. Nashville, Tennessee. All rights reserved.

"Is It the Truth?" by Leslie E. Duncan is reprinted from *Home Life.*

"It's a Start" by Gary Smalley and John Trent is reprinted from *Leaving the Light On: Building the Memories That Will Draw Your Kids Home,* © 1994 by Gary Smalley and John Trent. Used by permission of WaterBrook Multnomah, an imprint of the Crown Publishing Group, a division of Random House, Inc.

"Learning to Love" by Bernie "Richie" Thomassen (as told to Heather Black) is reprinted from *Chicken Soup for the Christian Teenage Soul,* edited by Jack Canfield, Mark Victor Hansen, Kimberly Kirberger, Patty Aubery, and Nancy Mitchell-Autio. Copyright © 2002 by Heather Black. Reprinted with the permission of Health Communications, Inc., www.hcibooks.com.

"Lessons from a Wallet" by Bruce McIver is reprinted by permission from *Stories I Couldn't Tell When I Was a Pastor,* 1991, Thomas Nelson, Inc. Nashville, Tennessee. All rights reserved.

"Look, Daddy, I Can Fly!" from *Still Lickin' the Spoon* and "I'm Daddy's Girl" from *Marriage 911* are reprinted by permission of the author Becky Freeman.

"My Dad" by Charles Swindoll is reprinted from *Come Before Winter.* Copyright by Charles Swindoll. Published by Zondervan Publishing.

"The Oak Tree" by Max Lucado is reprinted with permission from *No Wonder They Call Him Savior,* 2004, Thomas Nelson, Inc., Nashville, Tennessee. All rights reserved.

"Sizzle" by Margaret McSweeney, "Next Summer—on the Ice!" by Laurele Riipa, "The Voice of a Good Man" by Kristin Andress, "A Lullaby" by Deanna Allen, "A MillionMillion" by Debi Stack, "My Gift from Dad" by Steve Dwinnells, "My Father's Christmas" by Crystal Ward Kent, "My Father's Flag" by Kathryn Slattery, "Full Circle" by Janna L. Graber, "Not All Valentine's Come in Envelopes" by Robin Jones Gunn, "Al's Used Cars" by Lonnie Hull DuPont, "Between the Lines" by Charlotte Adelsperger, and "Wake-Up Call" by Bob Welch are reprinted with permission of the authors.

"Stick Shift" and "Yerr Out!" by Clark Cothern are from *At the Heart of Every Great Father,* copyright © 1998 by Clark Cothern. Used by permission of WaterBrook Multnomah, an imprint of Crown Publishing Group, a division of Random House, Inc.

(Acknowledgments continued from pages iv and 211)

"Taken for Granted" by Donna Pennington is from *Chicken Soup for the Father & Daughter Soul,* edited by Jack Canfield, Mark Victor Hansen, Patty Aubery, Nancy Mitchell-Autio, and Le-Ann Thiemann. Copyright © 2002 by Donna Pennington. Reprinted with permission of Health Communications, Inc., www.hcibooks.com.

"The Toolbox" by Joshua Harris is reprinted from *I Kissed Dating Good-bye: A New Attitude Toward Relationships and Romance*, copyright © 1997, 2003 by Joshua Harris. Used by permission of WaterBrook Multnomah, an imprint of Crown Publishing Group, a division of Random House, Inc.

"Where Are You Paddling ?" by George Walther is reprinted from *Chicken Soup for the Single Parent's Soul,* edited by Jack Canfield, Mark Victor Hansen, Laurie Hartman, and Nancy Vogl. Copyright © 2003 by George Walther. Reprinted with the permission of Health Communications, Inc., www. hcibooks.com.